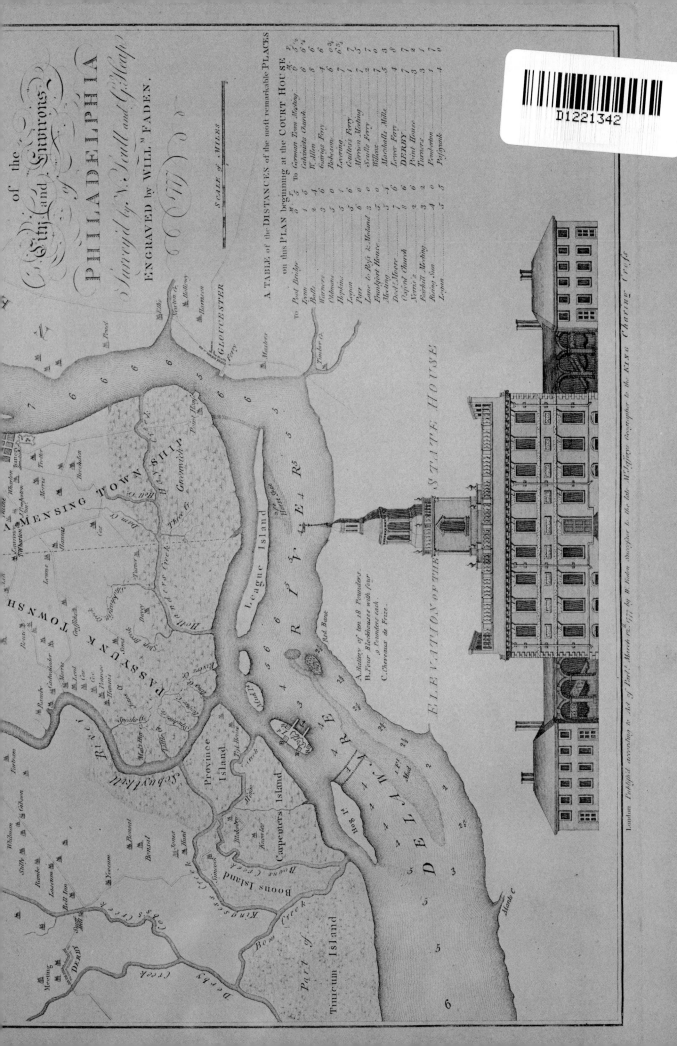

A Plan of the City and Environs of PHILADELPHIA

Surveyd by N. Scull and G. Heap

ENGRAVED by WILL.ᵐ FADEN.

(1777)

SCALE of MILES

A TABLE of the DISTANCES of the most remarkable PLACES on this PLAN beginning at the COURT HOUSE

To Point Bridge	0	5
Ivon	1	1
Bulls	2	4
Warners	3	0
Osbatus	4	5
Hopkins	5	3
Lagun	5	5
Parr	6	0
Lane to Byls & Moland	6	3
Frankfort House	5	5
Moring	6	7
Doct Moor	7	6
Oxford Church	8	0
Norris's	9	2
Fairhill Meeting	9	4
Rising Sun	4	2
Logan	4	5

To German Town Meeting	6	3
Cabenists Church	8	0
W. Allen	4	6
Garrips Ferry	6	0
Robeson	7	0
Levering	7	2
Goulteis Ferry	7	5
Merrion Meeting	7	5
Svalls Ferry	7	0
Willcox	8	1
Marshalls Mills	5	5
Lower Ferry	4	0
DERBY	7	0
Point House	3	1
Turners	3	2
Pemberton	1	0
Passyunk	2	0

STATE HOUSE

ELEVATION OF THE

A. Battery of ten 18 Pounders.
B. Four Blockhouses with four 9 Pounders each.
C. Chereaux de Frize.

London Published according to Act of Parliamᵗ March 12ᵗʰ 1777 by Wᵐ Faden Successor to the late Mᵗ Jefferys Geographer to the KING Charing Cross

PHILADELPHIA

THE UNEXPECTED CITY

PHILADELPHIA
THE UNEXPECTED CITY

Text and Pictures by

LAURENCE LAFORE

and

SARAH LEE LIPPINCOTT

1965

DOUBLEDAY & COMPANY, INC., GARDEN CITY, NEW YORK

PHILADELPHIA EDITION

CONTENTS

PREFACE

Two photographers in a city of two million people cannot see many of its representative or rewarding scenes. The authors claim no approach to omniscience, ubiquity, or prudence of selection. Our only authority derives from total lack of perspective; we are both natives, one born within and another upon the edge of Philadelphia, both lifelong residents, and—if a feeling for a city is inheritable—both descended from people who arrived in the neighborhood of Philadelphia two hundred and seventy-five years ago. We share the peculiarities of Philadelphians—including, as the alien reader may observe, a tendency to be mildly obsessed by the City Hall.

The pictures in this book were taken over a period of five years. They include a few buildings that have since been torn down, most notably and deplorably Frank Furness's Provident Trust Company. They exclude a great deal that we should have liked to include. Some things were left out because of ignorance; others, like Franklin's grave, because they proved unphotographable; and others simply for reasons of space. Among the many aspects of Philadelphia unrecorded here we particularly regret Powelton, a sinister slum now reclaimed as a stately, and racially integrated, community of tree-lined streets and Victorian villas; Saint Joseph's and Saint George's churches; Stenton, Solitude, and the Woodlands, fine eighteenth-century houses now surrounded by the city; John Bartram's house and garden; the beautiful University Museum; and the extraordinary Smith Memorial in Fairmount Park.

The suburbs were arbitrarily excluded. Within the city, the largest omission is Germantown. It has been incorporated in Philadelphia for more than a century, but it was founded, by German Quakers, as a separate town, and it is nearly as rich in old houses and old memories as central Philadelphia. Germantown deserves a volume of its own; the inclusion of occasional bits of it would be an impertinence. In general we have stayed close to the center of the city, with excursions to Manayunk, Kensington, and Frankford, and in one case a few hundred yards across the city line to the seminary of Saint Charles Borromeo in Merion. The only excuses for this violation of our rule are that the church of Saint Charles's is beautiful and that it can, at least, be clearly seen by someone standing within the city limits.

We are grateful for three photographs given us by Miss Marjorie Ferguson, of New York, and three by Mr. Steven Izenour, of New Haven, to whom we are also indebted for work in the darkroom. And we wish to thank the distinguished historian of colonial Philadelphia, Professor Frederick Tolles, and the distinguished Philadelphia architect, Mr. H. Mather Lippincott, Jr., for reading the manuscript and suggesting corrections and improvements.

SLL and LL

INTRODUCTION

In the summer of 1776 fifty-six British subjects in Philadelphia put their signatures to treason, forswore allegiance to their rightful sovereign King George the Third, defied the might of the British Empire, and delivered a new nation and the most powerful idea of their age. Their action was exceedingly daring. As Benjamin Franklin crisply remarked, "Gentlemen, we must all hang together, or assuredly we shall all hang separately."

The town in which their perilous resolution was taken was the metropolis of British North America and, by their decision, the capital of the United States. Even by the measure of the New World, it was a young city. It had been founded less than a century earlier, on the wooded ridge between two rivers that the Unami tribe called Coaquanock —the place of the tall pine—near the settlements on the Delaware where Swedes and Dutchmen had earlier fought to found empires for their mother countries. Boston and New York were its seniors by fifty years or more; the splendors of the Spanish capital on Lake Texcoco had flourished for a century and a half before the first bricks were laid in Philadelphia.

It had, however, grown prodigiously since its founding. By 1776 it was the greatest seaport and market of North America, and its cultural center. It was by any measure one of the great cities of the British Empire, if not second in population to London, then certainly third. And it lay, the keystone of the arch of the Atlantic seaboard, near the center of the thirteen colonies. Its choice as a meeting place for the Continental Congress had been dictated not only by its primacy but by its location.

The colonies, partly and rather sullenly united in their

dislike of British impositions, were united in little else. In 1776 conflicts among them were more numerous and scarcely less bitter than conflicts between them and the government at London. Pennsylvania and Connecticut were at war in the Wyoming Valley, a token of hostilities among thirteen provinces of widely various composition. Each colony, moreover, was itself divided on the great issues of the day. It had been the recent victory of the Scots-Irish in backwoods Pennsylvania over the conservative Quakers, Anglicans, and Germans of Philadelphia that had turned the tide in the province for defiance and independence and against accommodation.

Philadelphia was inclined to Toryism, at least in its merchant aristocracy. Nonetheless the traditions of the city were libertarian, and they proved infectious to members of the Congress and to the new nation. In face of drastic differences and dissensions, it was in the likeness of those traditions that the republic was made. Penn's vision of the brotherhood of man for which he had named his city had implanted in its soil diversity as well as freedom. The triumph of the backwoodsmen was the token of its power. Pennsylvania, splendidly tolerant, had received the widest assortment of races, faiths, and nationalities, as the nation was later to receive them. It had enjoyed for seventy-five years a charter that guaranteed their freedom. It had evolved an open society, never harmonious but exceedingly robust, where conflicting consciences and interests subsisted side by side in liberty.

In most of the other colonies, though each had developed its own notion of liberty, the notions of toleration and diversity were notably absent. The American provinces were not, in their nature, fit ancestors of a melting pot, or of a society of free men. Not New England, with its ferocious dedication to a dogma that had led within living memory to the hanging of witches and dissenters. Not New York, where the great patricians of the Hudson nurtured a society more nearly medieval than anything in England. Not the South, where landed gentlemen tranquilly superintended the toil of their Negroes. Most of the colonies had been founded in the interest of religious freedom, but only for subscribers to their individual heresies. Only in Pennsylvania was the founding sect one that on principle denied the goal of religious unity and the wickedness of aliens. When Saint Joseph's Church was built, in 1733, Philadelphia was the only place in the British Empire where a Roman Catholic Mass could be publicly celebrated. There was a good deal of prejudice, but when Saint Joseph's was threatened with sacking by an angry mob, Quakers formed a patrol to protect it.

The core of the American tradition was to be diversity, religious freedom, and the equality of human beings, and these were ideals that had been made in Philadelphia. The city was, then, in several senses the nation's birthplace; so it has always presented itself, and so today it invites the interest of all Americans. But it is also in many respects startlingly individual, and this individuality is the product of past primacy, but of primacy lost. It possesses, for those who see it that way, the romantic quality of diminished grandeur.

Most cities—and most societies, for that matter—that are in a state of pre-eminence and rapid growth, as Philadelphia was in 1776, tend either to further development toward a larger pre-eminence or to decay. The peculiar quality of

Philadelphia is that neither—or rather both—of these tendencies developed. Philadelphia grew steadily, even spectacularly, larger and richer. It maintained a degree of vitality that permitted its adjustment to changing economic demands and self-renewal after long periods of political corruption and lethargy. It has certainly not decayed. But it early lost its pre-eminence—as a political capital, to Harrisburg and Washington, as the American metropolis, to New York, whose proximity has accentuated its provinciality. In size it slipped from first to second, then third, and now fourth place.

The facts of simultaneous growth and decline, combined with its age and its location, have exerted upon Philadelphians a curiously conservative effect. Its past is pickled in its present. Chicago, Los Angeles, Houston were being born when Philadelphia had for a long time ceased to be pre-eminent; they have no heritage of diminished grandeur with all its haunting memories. Its successor, New York, has been the national headquarters for considerably more than a hundred years, an ample period to permit its well-known dynamism to destroy most surviving vestiges of its less splendid past. But in Philadelphia accumulating riches and population were bred in a setting where old ideas and—compared to New York anyway—buildings were cherished, a breeding it shared with Boston, Baltimore, and Charleston. Among American cities these four possess the qualities of junior, transatlantic Romes. But Philadelphia contrasts as sharply to them as to New York and Chicago. Unlike Boston, it never tasted the fruit or suffered the loss of an intellectual greatness, short-lived but dazzling. For a hundred years it has been characterized by an outward intellectual dowdiness, which conceals an inward intellectual stability. Unlike Baltimore it has become a giant, outgrowing its boundaries to become the center of a vast and growing region of suburbs and industrial towns.

Philadelphia is full of paradox. It appears to the casual visitor recalcitrantly philistine. It cannot match the intellectual tradition of New England. But it was the site of a prodigious series of cultural innovations: in it were founded the nation's first parks (the New England commons were for cows, not people), first hospital, first medical school, first observatory, first learned society, first daily newspaper, first academy of art, first scientific museum, first insurance company, first theater, as well as the first men's social club—the remarkable State-in-Schuylkill—organized anywhere including London. It has produced a constellation of names of great importance in the history of American writing, drama, and art. Among them, the journalist Richard Harding Davis; the novelist Owen Wister; the painter Thomas Eakins; the editor Edward Bok; the playwright Clifford Odets; the Barrymores on the stage. Its private collections—in particular, unexpectedly, collections of modern and contemporary art—are peculiarly rich. But only when their proprietors die and bequeath them to museums does the world at large learn about them. Aside from the Philadelphia Orchestra, the city's culture is usually secreted behind tightly closed doors.

Its conservatism is even more recalcitrant than its air of philistinism. The residents, at least the older ones, still call city blocks "squares" and sidewalks "pavements." And yet, in its urban experiments, it is uniquely daring. Its pride and consciousness of its past as the nation's birthplace are matched by what was, until recently, an incredibly negligent and materialistic view of its treasures. Next to New York, it is the most cosmopolitan of American cities; it is also the most parochial. It possesses both deplorable slums and an incredible quantity and diversity of institutions of higher education. In its long history of obstinate devotion to small-town habits, to single-family dwellings, to galaxies of obscure little shops, to the worst restaurants in the nation, it has spasmodically surrendered, on a grandiose scale, to the customs of more lively cities—imitation Champs Elysées, skyscrapers, apartment houses, and neon lighting.

Behind these surrenders the paradoxes reflect themselves in a peculiar and characteristic quality of life, unseen by outsiders and unnoticed by most Philadelphians. This quality is imponderable and intangible, but it possesses material symptoms which may be photographed and, suitably juxtaposed, may give some suggestions of the life of the city. They cannot show much of its curious flavor, any more than they can record its special physical atmosphere, the alternating phases of clarity and mist that cloak the skyline in sparkling reflections and then, a few minutes later, in a pink haze. They cannot suggest the tenor of its ways, unself-conscious, complacent, and easy, summarized in small ambitions and an inclination to go early to bed.

Philadelphians have little to stay awake for—there are few night clubs, and those few uninteresting. There is nothing to regret and nothing to overtake. Of all American cities it is the quietest, the most poised, and the most mature. It is uniquely skilled at absorbing disparate elements, and for that it is to those who see it with a fresh eye the most unexpected of cities.

The World They Brought:
Splendors and Simplicities

PART ONE

The Quakers of Pennsylvania opened their province to men and women of diverse nations and religions. Their generosity proved their undoing so far as control of the new land went; they were eventually outnumbered in it and lost control of the government. But in their brief tenure they had impressed their mark upon the province, and their heirs were so numerous that none of them ever won dominance. Pennsylvania was so varied that it could survive only by continued toleration.

Long before the rest of America became the haven for a cosmopolitan crowd of immigrants, Pennsylvania was settled by Welshmen, Germans, Dutchmen, Irishmen, and Scots, followed by a rising tide of Poles, Russians, Chinese, and Greeks—and by Negroes, honorably received as refugees from servitude in the South, not ignobly seized and sold from their homelands. Anglicans, Jews, Methodists, Catholics and Presbyterians were rubbing elbows in Philadelphia before the American Revolution, and in the farms beyond there were smaller and stranger sects, Amish, Mennonites, Schwenkfelders and Moravians. The city and the countryside raised spires, which Quakers disdained, to varied deities.

The cosmopolitanism was that of little people. Philadelphia was, as it is today, a federation of villages, and many of the villages were nations, the seats of transplanted traditions. They flourished, and some of them have survived. There are a hundred exotic corners: in the Ninth Street Market; in precipitous Manayunk, as Umbrian in its aspect as it is Indian in its name; in Polish Richmond; in Kensington which was settled by the English and where cricket is still played, although the population is now largely Eastern European; in Fairmount, now Puerto Rican, with its Spanish street signs. Here, hybridized but persisting, the Americans' origins are revealed. A hundred cities have had the same character, but most of them have it no longer, or only in traces; their citizens have destroyed it as they fought for assimilation. Unity in diversity, the Quakers' hope and dream, survived in Philadelphia in place of the aspiration of uniformity.

The immigrant communities were made of ordinary citizens; they were the architects of democracy. But they dignified their villages with monuments built to the glory of God. In contrast to their Quaker hosts, who not only insisted upon simplicity in their places of worship but showed no concern to preserve them once built, the new arrivals constructed grandly and cherished their churches. Saint Joseph's and Saint Augustine's are among the oldest Roman Catholic churches in the country; Saint George's is the oldest Methodist church, and Christ Church and Saint Peter's among the oldest Anglican churches. Most of them were simple enough, but imposing compared to the Quaker meetinghouses, and they formed the dominant feature of the early skyline, a tangible tribute to toleration.

It was odd, and appropriate, that the churches, so diverse in liturgy and in the origins of their congregations, should show a character so strongly English in their architecture, as a compensating tribute to the authors of freedom. The tradition curiously persists; a German Lutheran church built in purest Georgian is a singular exemplification of the melting pot.

As Philadelphia was welcoming the various creeds and cultures, money accumulated. Merchants, bankers, lawyers, doctors, farmers, and those characteristic eighteenth-century figures who tried their hands, often with great success, at a diversity of business enterprises and cultural endeavors, were growing rich. They contributed enthusiastically to civic enterprises; they built fine homes for the hospitals and libraries they supported, and for themselves as well. Many of them also built country houses, the Logans at Stenton, the Chews at Cliveden, the Morrises at Lemon Hill, the Hamiltons at Woodlands, the Penns at Lansdowne and Solitude. The finest views and favorite sites stretched along the Schuylkill, and here there arose a remarkable series of houses surrounded by gardens, orchards, and farms. These country seats have often erroneously been called manors—manorial rights were unknown in Pennsylvania—or, no less erroneously, mansions. Although the scale was sometimes manorial, they were simply residences convenient to the city, the handsome forerunners of suburban villas.

In the nineteenth century came much greater wealth, and the abandonment of republican simplicity. Secular splendors proliferated, borrowed now, not brought, from the Old World. The mansions of the rich, the stores of the merchants, the egregious City Hall, represented no continuation of an old tradition but incongruous imitations of it. The standard of perfection for urban prospects became, progressively, the Paris of the Place de la Concorde. Philadelphia set out to re-create such perfections, haphazardly and with liberal interpretations at first, then with a burst of academic resolution that culminated in the monumental prospect of the

Frankford Friends Meeting House

Christ Church spire

Parkway and the Art Museum, built in the 1920s. Bankers, impressed properly enough by the origins of their profession in Renaissance Florence, reproduced at the corner of Fifteenth and Walnut streets the edifice in which Florentine bankers had been housed.

The age of borrowed splendors died in depression. After the nineteen-thirties no one dreamed of trying to build another Florence or another Paris on the Schuylkill. But the older cosmopolitanism survives, its simpler forms more deeply rooted, in the life of the city and, here and there, in an outward sign.

The Quakers who founded Philadelphia and made it their enormous monument have left no traces of their early building. The first meetinghouses were soon demolished. Their replacements, however, amply demonstrate the Friends' avoidance of worldly extravagance, whether in deportment or architecture. Frankford Friends Meeting, in north Philadelphia, resembles as nearly as possible a frame farmhouse.

More substantial monuments to their ideals are the churches—steeple-houses, the Friends called them—that their tolerance permitted to the dissenting faiths that found a welcome in their city. The Church of England, opposed to Quakerism on this as on most points, believed that churches should testify to the glory of God rather than the modesty of man, and in Christ Church, begun in 1727, the Anglicans gave to Philadelphia its first taste of architectural splendor and its first and most beautiful spire. In successful competition with skyscrapers a few squares away, Christ Church still dominates the Delaware waterfront, a testimony to Quaker tolerance, to the growing wealth of the city, and to the incomparable architectural tradition it inherited.

5

The Friends Meeting Houses of central Philadelphia, all of them built in the ninteenth century, are hidden in dark courtyards among tall buildings, like the Race Street Meeting, here seen from across the street through the grille of a modern hospital. A rather similar effect is provided by a tree, gnarled and stunted in the interests of art, in front of the Japanese House in Fairmount Park, a twentieth-century acquisition that may be taken as a token of the Quakers' continued ecumenical hospitality to exotic cultures. Few Japanese, however, came to Philadelphia; a much greater strain on the tolerance of the Quakers was imposed by the Anglicans, Calvinists, and Roman Catholics, who soon outnumbered them. After Christ Church, the Anglicans shortly required additional parishes, and two more churches, Saint Peter's and then Saint Paul's, were built before the Revolution, the latter of them in 1761. Roman Catholicism grew even faster. A hundred years after the first Catholic church

6

Cathedral of SS. Peter and Paul, Logan Circle

was built, plans were being made for the splendid cathedral of SS. Peter and Paul on Logan Square, whose architecture is in a tradition as Roman as that of the archbishop whose throne it contains, and whose opulent immensity forms as sharp a contrast to the nearby Race Street Meeting as Catholic doctrine to Quaker beliefs.

Jews were also prominent—and free to practice their religion—from the early years of the city. Mikveh Israel Cemetery, on Spruce Street at Darien, is on land granted to Rabbi Nathan Levy by John Penn and was the burying ground of the earliest Jewish Congregation, organized in 1747. The Jewish community was eminent in the patriotic cause after 1776; much earlier its members had figured on the first list of the Philadelphia Assembly, founded in 1748, and their descendants are still members of this oldest and most aristocratic of subscription dances.

8

Saint Paul's Episcopal Church, S. Third Street

Mikveh Israel Cemetery, Spruce Street beyond Eighth

9

Strawberry Mansion, Fairmount Park East

While creeds and churches were proliferating, the great
men of Philadelphia were energetically building country
houses, at distances convenient to the town but safely remote from its summer effluvia. The most elegant of them, on
the Schuylkill hills, became uninhabitable when the spreading town's need for reliable water required the damming of
the river, which produced an intolerable infestation of
mosquitoes and obliged the original proprietors to decamp.
The city, in an unusual burst of farsightedness, began to
buy them up to add to Fairmount Park, and they survive
today in admirable repair and in their original rural setting.

At the end of the eighteenth century Judge William Lewis,
a friend of Washington and a leading figure in the city, built
a Georgian house on what was later called Strawberry Hill.

10

Corner grocery, Manayunk

It was eventually expanded with wings of a naïve but charming Italian design. After being used as a dairy farm, a beer garden, a police court, and a brothel, it was restored by a commendable organization called the Committee of 1926.

Within sight of Strawberry Mansion, a few miles upstream, is the river town of Manayunk. Now part of the city, it grew up in the early nineteenth century as a factory town and port, neatly demonstrating the transition from an economy of Anglo-Saxon landowners and merchants to one of mills staffed by immigrants from the Continent. Even in the simplicities of Manayunk, however, the imported inspiration that made Strawberry Mansion into an Italianate villa shows itself in Italianate details and the still more

11

Saint Augustine's,
Fourth and New streets

Italianate atmosphere of sun-washed drowsiness of a corner grocery store.

Another note of unity may be faintly heard, although at second hand. The Quakers, avoiding all forms of idolatry, named their streets and houses for native trees and fruits and so set a fashion for half the place names in the nation. Strawberry Mansion, although its name dates from much later than its building, is in the tradition; the grocery store is at the corner of Grape and Silverwood streets.

The dissenting settlers of the early years clung to the Georgian vernacular for their churches. The second Roman

City Hall from East Market Street

Catholic parish church was Saint Augustine's, built soon after the Revolution at Fourth and New streets with the conventional simplicity inherited from Christopher Wren. A generation later more lavish tastes submerged the Wren tradition, and William Strickland, the brilliant and highly disciplined neoclassicist, suffered an attack of inventiveness and added a peculiar cupola. Another generation passed; the descendants of Wren had forgotten and forsworn their heritage, and an even more inventive architect built City Hall tower, crowned by a huge dome that visibly suggests the influence of Strickland's whimsy.

13

East Portico, Art Museum

The Quakers were so strongly opposed to paganism that they refused to call the days of the week and the months of the year by names like Saturday or August and used instead the uninteresting terms, Seventh Day and Eighth Month. But newcomers to Pennsylvania brought with them the habit of a sound classical education, and at the end of the eighteenth century the men of the early republic were finding in Athenian democracy a congenial ideological homeland, and in the cool perfection of Athenian temples appropriate models for their own classical age. The passion for pagan prototypes was fostered in Philadelphia by the Aristotelians of the Continental Congress and the designs of Benjamin Latrobe. It rapidly became national, and the Congress eventually moved to Latrobe's Capitol at Washington, but nowhere did neoclassicism prove more fruitful or more durable than in Philadelphia. In the 1920s it was to produce the Art Museum, with its magnificent portico; a hundred years earlier, in the hands of John Haviland, it had shaped the smaller but not dissimilar portico of the Episcopal Church of Saint Andrew.

Saint George's Greek Orthodox Church, S. Eighth Street

Greek shop signs, Locust Street at Eighth

Saint Andrew's has since been reconsecrated to Saint George and the cult of the Greek Orthodox Church, to serve the descendants of ancient Athenians whose shop signs mark their community around the corner. The communicants, and Haviland's Ionic columns, provide an unexpected link among the very different heirs of a single civilization, separated for two thousand years and then reunited in Phila·delphia.

Not only Federalists and Greek immigrants descended from the Periclean Age; nineteenth-century German Lutherans were no less its heirs, and their church too bears the pagan imprint.

Door of German St. Paul's Evangelical Lutheran Church, N. American and Brown streets

Gloria Dei

Saint John the Baptist, Manayunk

18

Cheese stall, Reading Terminal Market

Spanish street sign, Green Street

The unexpected fruit of Quaker toleration was a cosmopolitan society. But indeed Philadelphia was cosmopolitan from its birth; Penn's followers found on their arrival the remnants of an earlier attempt at colonization by the Swedes, and although New Sweden lost its name and dynasty, the Swedish settlers flourished in the English colony. In 1698 Swedish Lutherans set out to build a new church, one that faithfully recalled the village churches of the homeland. Its congregation was in time absorbed by the larger influx of Anglicans; Old Swedes', as it is still called, became officially the Episcopal Church of Gloria Dei, and the building was much altered. But it still stands on a street named Swanson, the oldest church in Philadelphia, and the stiff gables and small belfry, the shaded churchyard with an occasional glimpse of masts in the Delaware, still recall both its Swedish forebears and the rustic village in which it once stood, now otherwise lost in a mournful waterfront slum.

From the other end of Europe a richer and more dramatic civilization supplied the splendors of Saint John the Baptist, rising finely above the Schuylkill at Manayunk. Its beautiful spire and theatrical location, the terraced park in front, convey its associations with the Mediterranean instead of the Baltic, with the sprawling opulence of a Latin city instead of the tidy simplicities of rural Scandinavia.

The cosmopolitanism persists, with cultures united but not fused. In the stalls of Reading Terminal Market are displayed wares to gratify a diversity of tastes in cheese ancestrally formed in a dozen foreign lands.

Philadelphia's variety is as remarkable in the degree of success with which its components have adapted themselves to transplantation as in the profusion of its sources. Unexpectedly, the Japanese House settles with ease and rightness into the alien landscape of Fairmount Park. But Italian

20

Da Vinci Restaurant, Walnut beyond Twenty-first Street

Italian-language billboard, Passyunk Avenue

wines, and their advertising, have suffered a sea change, and a sidewalk café, the only one in the city, grimly persisting behind piles of dirty snow, illustrates the difficulty of transferring the Latin way of life to a cold climate.

Woodford, Fairmount Park East

Merchants, bankers, and judges were the great men of colonial Philadelphia. They lived in great houses whose most ostentatious features were their doorways. In 1756 Judge William Coleman rebuilt Woodford, in the favored region on the hills by the Schuylkill and provided it with one of the finest of the classical doorways that contemporary Philadelphians have inherited from their ancestors. Today one of the inheritors sits disconsolately in another doorway, grander if less handsome than Woodford's and surmounted by the arms of the city, which here paternally assures its citizens an opportunity to enjoy the blessings of cleanliness through the provision of public baths. On a more humble doorstep, other inheritors relax in a less morose mood.

Child on steps of Public Baths

Children on doorstep

Benjamin Franklin Parkway and City Hall

The passion for splendor, like a recurrent fever, seized Philadelphia at intervals. In the 1860s it took the form of City Hall; fifty years later it reappeared in plans for a monumental boulevard cutting diagonally through the squalid gridiron to the Fairmount and modeled on the Champs Elysées. It was planned by a Frenchman named Jacques Gréber, whose grasp on the needs of a twentieth-century American city was stupefyingly weak. The scale and the prospects it opened are magnificent, but its chief functional consequence, aside from traffic jams, has been the isolation from daily life or easy access of the libraries, museums, and art galleries for which it was intended to serve as an approach. And Gréber's Champs Elysées left the surrounding slums untouched; now they are being gradually replaced by huge and dreary apartment houses that dwarf his conception.

26

Ninth Street Market

But the periodic mania for Parisian vistas passed most Philadelphians by. Disregarding the great avenue closed by the dome of City Hall, they continued to live and do their business in the narrow alleys that Penn had decreed, in small shops and open markets like that on South Ninth Street, where the prospect is also closed by a cupola, small but reminiscent, and the flavor is more surely foreign than any Gréber achieved.

Except when motor-driven, natives shun the inaccessible reaches of the Parkway. Their diversions, like their business, are conducted in less overpowering settings, and very often at the edges of the rivers, creeks, fountains and pools that so liberally water the city's open spaces. The fisherman on the Schuylkill, sleepily unexpectant of results, is far more Parisian in mood than the factitious boulevard.

27

Boat House Row and Lemon Hill

Fisherman on Schuylkill embankment

Children at pool in Rittenhouse Square

Mount Pleasant, east front

Mount Pleasant, west front

Fruit vendor, Delaware Avenue

Fishmongers, Ninth Street Market

From Boat House Row, against the background of Lemon Hill with its Georgian villa, Thomas Eakins's oarsmen set out in their sculls, and an Irish bricklayer named John Kelly trained with the Penn crew. He was the greatest of American rowers, but he was excluded from the Henley Regatta, by a committee of genteel Englishmen, on the ground of his working-class origin. A generation afterward the Queen of England, observing the etiquette of reigning monarchs, would be obliged to address John Kelly's daughter as her cousin of Monaco.

A local counterpart of this American drama is illustrated in Rittenhouse Square, the stronghold and synonym of Philadelphia's own dynasts. Today, in its pool, the unconscious heirs of an aristocratic past go wading.

The most beautiful of the country houses along the river, and perhaps the most beautiful private house in America, is Mount Pleasant. It was built in the 1760s by a Scots sea captain named M'Pherson, who sold it to Benedict Arnold as a wedding present for his bride, Peggy Shippen. The Arnolds were prevented, by the outbreak of war and by a small matter of side changing, from living in it. It was confiscated by the Commonwealth, and eventually opened as a museum. With its graceful outbuildings, its fine garden, and its view of the city across open fields it strongly evokes the idyls of the eighteenth century, in which the very rich and very cultivated men and women of a golden age conducted passionate, decorous intrigues, both amorous and political, to the tune of minuets.

While such stately affairs were enacted in great houses, busier and less cultivated Philadelphians bought and sold and proved the merits of Poor Richard's sententious dictum that a penny saved was a penny earned. They still do; Mount Pleasant, empty of all save ghosts, stands lonely on its hilltop, but on Ninth Street fishmongers still deal in a market like those of Peggy Shippen's day, and on Delaware Avenue, near the little harbor where Penn's ship first touched Philadelphia, a fruit vendor purveys his wares to passing pedestrians.

The splendors of Mount Pleasant were conceived by a native ruling class in an architectural tradition naturalized, like themselves, by several generations in America. The temptation to borrow grew on their descendants and culminated in an orgy of imitations. Italy and France seemed indefinably *more* splendid than Pennsylvania or England. The bank building at Fifteenth and Walnut effectively demonstrated the solidity of its finances in a replica of the Florentine Palazzo Strozzi. It is the most imposing commercial example of Old-World borrowing in the center of the city, but not one pedestrian in a thousand looks up from the pavement to enjoy the tour of the Tuscan Renaissance that the bankers have provided for him free of cost.

At the edge of the city, immigrants were also building, unself-consciously and perhaps unconsciously, in European ways. In Grape Street, Manayunk, characteristic of dozens of streets like it, only the double-hung sashes and the white pointing could tell a visitor he was in America. Discovered

Bank building, Fifteenth and Walnut streets

Grape Street, Manayunk

Norris Square

now by artists, Manayunk still composedly exercises the potent charm of authenticity, of an unintended continuity from the culture its inhabitants brought with them.

Penn's original plan for Philadelphia called for five large open squares geometrically distributed through the rectangle of streets, and named Northwestern Square, Southeastern Square, and so on. They were to provide centers of greenery

Free Library and Municipal Court Building

and wholesome recreation for the residents of the low brick
houses that would eventually surround them. Today the
atmosphere that he must have imagined, and even the sort of
houses, are to be found only in the nineteenth-century
squares that were built much later following his plan, in
neighborhoods many miles beyond the boundaries that Penn

37

fixed. They help to preserve some of flavor of what he called his green country town. One of the pleasantest is Norris Square, far to the northeast of Penn's city.

The five original squares, equipped with less uncompromising names, have largely lost the quality that persists in the outer city. Center Square, renamed for Penn, is entirely occupied by City Hall. Rittenhouse and Washington are shadowed by skyscraper apartments. Franklin is divided between the approaches of the Delaware Bridge and the unsavory vestiges of Philadelphia's skid row. Logan became the center of the City Beautiful that Francophile planners of fifty years ago conceived to unite the park and the center of the city.

The two leading achievements of the City Beautiful are the Municipal Court Building and the Free Library, on the north side of what is now called Logan Circle. They are the most strictly academic of Philadelphia's imported splendors, being almost—not quite—facsimiles of Gabriel's twin palaces that face the Place de la Concorde. Pretentious, pointless, and very lovely, they face the sunken Vine Street Expressway and the dense foliage of the circle instead of the superb expanse of the Concorde, and they frame not the fine symmetries of the Rue Royale, closed by the Madeleine, but the dismal reaches of North Nineteenth Street. They are a good example of the recurrent impulse to build a new Paris on the Schuylkill and of the disastrous failure to reckon the relation between design and setting. Less than forty years old, they already have an air of neglect and melancholy, monuments to a cause long lost.

The World They Borrowed:
An Abundance of Golden Ages

PART TWO

Sometime in the fifteenth century Europeans discovered the ancient world and fell in love with it. Thereafter they abandoned their own architectural past, which had produced the glories of Chartres and Canterbury, to turn back to a distant legacy from Rome and Greece. In the end the rejection of their medieval inheritance was total; Gothic became, by the time the United States was being formed, a synonym for barbaric.

It was the classical tradition, remarkably long-lasting and adaptable, remarkably productive of fecund variations, that formed the inspiration for the buildings of colonial America and of the early republic. Only in the twentieth century has it lost its lure and its vitality, and even now an occasional country club or real estate office is reflexively equipped with Corinthian columns to provide a reminder of a great era. Generally speaking, Corinthian columns cost too much nowadays, and they are no longer acceptable to a sophisticated taste bred on the doctrine that form must be adjusted to function, and decoration eschewed.

The classical tradition was never, until its death throes, mechanical or rigid. On the contrary it was extraordinarily flexible, and each age and nation imprinted its own characteristic tastes upon it. Changing times and varying materials transformed it. It produced the remote cousins called Renaissance, Palladian, Georgian, Early American, and Federal, which have little in common except their ancestor in Attica.

In the early nineteenth century the taste for imitation broadened and the taste for innovation flowered. Greek temples, judiciously amended to the needs of banking, government, or Christianity, continued to be constructed, but the

virtues of other models were suddenly discerned, and reproduced. The Mycenaean Age was much admired, and so was ancient Egypt. Medieval Gothic, so much despised by the generation of the founding fathers, was brought across the ocean in forms and materials that would have dazed its makers by their variety and ineptness. Then the French and the Italian Renaissance found their followers, and finally in the 1890s Americans began to imitate their own past, the eighteenth-century Georgian buildings that form the finest of our architectural survivals. Neo-Georgian designs—"colonial," they were vaguely called—were often beautiful and were certainly better adapted to the requirements of schools and filling stations than were medieval cathedrals, but they were often lifelessly imitative, lacking the imagination and

The dormitories of the University of Pennsylvania

freedom of their prototypes. They were the last and most sterile, if by no means the ugliest, of the surviving "styles" from the past.

Perhaps more munificently than any other city in the world, Philadelphia is furnished—the metaphor is accurate—with a record of architectural fantasies of the past two hundred years. It is, as North American cities go, old, large, and rich. It has never equated demolition with virtue, as has New York. It has been freer than European cities, loaded with older architecture, to follow the whimsies of the nineteenth century. It contains an abundance of golden ages.

Here are prisons dressed as feudal castles. Here are innumerable specimens of the Italian Renaissance, loosely embodied in a Victorian "villa" or majestically reproduced in the seminary of Saint Charles Borromeo. Here is the French Renaissance, largely expanded and delicately touched with lunacy, in the City Hall. Here are the marvels of ancient Greece sedately seated behind the railings of Girard College. Here, enthroned above the Schuylkill, is its twentieth-century manifestation, the Philadelphia Museum of Art. Here is the Romanesque, fancifully distorted in a church on Green Street, and superbly so in the Masonic Temple. Here is the Gothic, romantically rendered in College Hall. Here is the Tudors' Hampton Court adapted to a men's dormitory. Here, for the cost of a bus ticket or a parking meter, is a tour among the masterpieces of European architecture, some whimsically interpreted, some oddly adjusted to incongruous requirements, some finely faithful to their inspiration.

41

West Gate, Moyamensing Prison

The Lion Gate of the city of Mycenae in southern Greece is the oldest surviving example of monumental architecture in Europe. It marks the beginning of Western civilization. In 1832 Thomas Walter designed the Philadelphia County Prison at Moyamensing and provided it with a portal along Mycenaean lines, omitting the lions—perhaps for reasons of economy, possibly because they seemed less appropriate to a jail than to a royal palace. The prison, like the neighborhood around it, has fallen on evil days and is destined for demolition. For the moment the massive souvenir of Agamemnon's city still stands and easily survives comparison with the most characteristic product of twentieth-century design, the automobile.

The next important European architecture after Mycenae was that of classical Greece. Five centuries before the birth of Christ, Greeks were building perhaps the hand-

Founder's Hall, Girard College

somest buildings the Western world has yet produced. They served as a model for the Romans and an inspiration to Europeans of the Renaissance and eighteenth century. Not until the birth of the American republic, however, did it occur to people to attempt facsimiles of Greek temples.

Of the numerous replicas that appeared in Philadelphia, the main building of Girard College is one of the most successful in recapturing the calm and dignity of the originals. Designed, surprisingly, by the same man responsible for the Mycenaean gate, and begun a year later, it is now surrounded by lawns and trees of an un-Hellenic lushness, but the impeccable Corinthian colonnades march in authentic majesty. It shares at least one other quality with a pagan temple: Stephen Girard, the Swiss-born financier by whose bequest the college was founded, left in his will instructions that no Christian clergyman should ever set foot within its

Ridgway Library

Wing of Philadelphia Museum of Art

gates. Girard was an eminent benefactor of Philadelphia, and it is probably the only American city in which has been commemorated—in a college, an important avenue, a bridge, a leading bank, a housing development, and a hotel—the name of a militant atheist.

Founder's Hall at Girard College is the purest Corinthian building in the city; the Philadelphia Museum of Art is the largest and handsomest Ionic one. Set on the rocks of the Fairmount, a faintly acropolitan eminence above the Schuylkill, surrounded with statuary and fountains, the Art Museum is marvelously stirring. The gifted architects achieved what so many imitators of Greece failed in—flawless proportion and vigorous originality.

The oldest of the classical orders, the Doric, is represented in the Ridgway Library, built in the eighteen-seventies for Franklin's Library Company, which had outgrown its original quarters near the State House. The new building was unfortunately located far from the center of town, on South Broad Street. Around it developed a neighborhood whose inhabitants were, in general, little inclined to bookishness. The library languished. It is now to be transferred to another site and the Doric temple is consigned to destruction. Its massive exterior consists of three separate temples rather clumsily conjoined; it is not the equal of its Corinthian or Ionic counterparts, but the proportions are just, and convey a truer sense of its model than most of the other classical porticoes scattered through the city.

Venetian town house

Art Museum, from City Hall tower

Bank at Second and Chestnut streets

The Art Museum, seen from City Hall tower, regally closes the long perspective of the Franklin Parkway and dominates its surroundings as much by excellence of design as by size.

The purely Greek buildings are much less common than imitations of the other periods which were themselves imitating, or at least adapting, classical prototypes. In many of these the classical influence appears at fourth or fifth hand. The kinship of the Art Museum and the flat-faced town house may at first appear obscure, but the house traces its ancestry through a Venetian palazzo to forebears in both Rome and Byzantium, and thence to Greece.

A more complicated genealogy, involving a good many common-law marriages, would be required for the bank building at Second and Chestnut streets. It seems to have ancestors in eighteenth-century England, in Austria of the rococo age, in Renaissance France, and in a good many other places. This is the classical tradition gone berserk; the most enduring tradition inherited from Greece was of dignified repose, equally evident in the Art Museum and its distant cousin the State House. Here there is wild exuberance; but the family resemblance, illegitimately borne, is still faintly visible among the sandstone garlands.

Of all the eras that borrowed from antiquity, the Italian Renaissance made the best use of it. Its engineers and artists never sank to copying. They made a new set of traditions from the old. Their buildings were more complex than those

47

Church of the seminary of Saint Charles Borromeo

Italianate villa, Forty-fifth Street and Haverford Avenue

of the ancient world, and perhaps for that reason lend themselves less well to reproduction. Most Renaissance and baroque buildings in Philadelphia are either sterile or fantastic. But there are exceptions.

The church of Saint Martin, in the seminary of Saint Charles Borromeo, built in 1928, recaptures with dazzling success the sleek glory of its prototype. At once stately and exhilarating, it might be standing on any Italian plain—an illusion assisted by the facsimile of a Roman pine tree in the foreground.

In contrasting mood is a forlorn, though scarcely less evocative, Italian villa in West Philadelphia, representative of hundreds of its kind that appeared in the decades after 1850. Their models, country houses of Latium or Umbria, were less fastidiously followed and more freely interpreted

Pegasus at Memorial Hall

Memorial Hall, Fairmount Park West

than that of Saint Martin's. But even with flaking white paint instead of the tawny orange of the originals, even in shabbiness and dereliction, the copies preserve a haggard dignity. And their inspiration is sufficiently authentic to convey to Philadelphians visiting Rome for the first time an eerie sense of *déjà vu*.

The greatest architect of late sixteenth-century Italy was Andrea Palladio, who admirably adapted ancient Roman designs to the needs of his age. His influence on English-speaking countries was prodigious and long-lived. Half the banks and schools in the United States owe something to him. In Philadelphia, the most impressive Palladian building is Memorial Hall. It was built as the art gallery of the Centennial Exposition in 1876 and for a long time continued to house a display of extremely poor nineteenth-century paintings. It has now been converted into a recreation center and gymnasium. Memorial Hall was exposition

Franklin Institute, Logan Circle

architecture at its most assertive, but it was undoubtedly imposing, and it gains greatly from its setting in Fairmount Park and from the splendid Pegasi that flank its portals.

The Franklin Institute, built on Logan Circle in the early nineteen-thirties, was intended to honor a genius of even greater scope and stature than Palladio. At the moment of its construction the classical tradition was finally, after two and a half fecund millennia, expiring of exhaustion and economic strangulation; the Franklin Institute suffers from a species of rigor mortis. Inside are displayed the wonders of twentieth-century science; disparity of form and function has rarely been more marked. The main portico has a sort of moribund majesty, but the building as a whole is a poor memorial to the most inventive mind of the eighteenth century—and to the oldest and richest tradition of Western civilization.

Widener House, Broad Street and Girard Avenue

By the middle of the sixteenth century the Italian Renaissance influence had spread to France and become naturalized in its inhospitable climate. The examples from the south were sometimes strictly adhered to and sometimes loosely interpreted in ungainly union with older French styles. Moats and turrets persisted as ornaments in an age when defense was no longer a serious need for country houses, and Gothic gargoyles hovered oddly at the edges of classical domes. Such hybrid forms were much favored in the decades after the Civil War by the very rich. The Wideners, the most successful of the late nineteenth-century Philadelphia tycoons, in 1887 built a medium-size château

52

French Renaissance doorway, Walnut Street near Twenty-first

for themselves at the corner of Broad Street and Girard Avenue, in a neighborhood that even then was unfashionable and is now much more unfashionable. The details of its conservatories and loggias are wildly eclectic, but the general outlines are those of a French *manoir* from the least disciplined period of French architecture.

The French Renaissance also supplied Philadelphia with a large number of details—oriels, lintels, doorways. They are often lost in a confusion of banalities, and passers-by rarely notice them, but they are frequently worth looking at. They form a gallery of charming exhibits from the age of the Valois, like this pleasant doorway to a house on Walnut Street.

Dormitory of the University of Pennsylvania, Spruce Street at Thirty-seventh

Across the Channel, some years after the Renaissance
flowered in France, arose an analogous style known as Tudor
or, in its later stages, Jacobean. A fusion of Italian details
and English traditions, richly embellished by an age of extreme self-assurance, it tended to awkwardness and self-
consciousness, but it was widely applied in this country to
suburban residences and college dormitories. In 1895 the
University of Pennsylvania began to build a series of quadrangles—not completed for forty years—and had the good
fortune to employ a firm of architects who not only under-
stood the style they were working with but were able to
improve on it. It was a rare achievement, and Penn under-
graduates are as a result housed in buildings that pleas-
antly combine reminiscences of Shakespearean England with
perfectly workable and unaffected practicality.

The most remarkable of Philadelphia's borrowings from
the French Renaissance was City Hall. It was planned in
the late sixties, in the flush aftermath of the Civil War,
and its construction lasted almost until the end of the century. From the beginning City Hall was a center of violent

debate. A strong campaign, fortunately ending in a victorious referendum, was fought by opponents of the original plan of building it in Independence Square, a proposal almost as unnerving as that of the king of Greece a few years earlier, to remodel the Parthenon as a royal residence. During the course of construction there were scandals and constant charges of unblushing graft as well as insane extravagance (the cost was twenty-six million dollars, which was certainly high). Scarcely was it completed when the public taste for lushness in architecture declined, and City Hall became a scandal of a different sort, a public joke. Some fifty years afterward the city fathers, tired of the staggering cost of maintaining a very inefficient office building, announced that they were going to tear it down. Philadelphians reacted with fury. Everyone had always made fun of it; now it turned out that everyone was deeply attached to it. The city fathers retreated; instead of demolishing it they decided to give it a good cleaning.

The results of the cleaning are extraordinary. It is probably the only non-controversial episode in the building's history. Radiant white stone and bluish slates have emerged from under the accumulation of dirt looking rather like a Wedgwood vase, revealing a striking, if peculiar, beauty.

City Hall was inspired, approximately, by the Tuileries Palace in Paris, and by adjacent portions of the Louvre. The Parisian models were masterpieces of French art; City Hall, foreshortened and much heightened, is a masterpiece of nothing except extravagance. Its abundance of ornament must originally have been stupefying, but now it is relatively chaste. In 1919 no less than twenty tons of ornamental stonework were removed out of concern for the safety of pedestrians passing below, and there have been further removals since. Still, a good deal remains—large figures crouched on pediments and cornices, wreathed pilasters, animals, birds, mottoes, and coats of arms. But if the profusion is somewhat overpowering, it is now possible to see that much of the sculpture has merit, including numerous works by Alexander Milne Calder, the first of three generations of famous Philadelphia sculptors.

Saint Francis Xavier,
Green Street at Twenty-third

In the Dark Ages, some seven hundred years before the
Renaissance burgeoned in France, Europe was beginning
to build in a fashion called Romanesque, which had developed out of the Roman tradition and, in a poorer and less
sophisticated age, salvaged something of Roman engineering skills while losing the flashiness of the later Empire. In
the nineteenth century Romanesque design was regarded
as appropriate to churches, schools, and banks, and occasionally to private houses. Its extreme massiveness was congenial to the Victorian generation, as were its intimations
of darkness and gloom, and its simplicity and straightfor-
wardness could easily be overcome by judicious amendment.

Even the best of the neo-Romanesque architects enriched
their buildings with fraudulent arrays of arcades and columns. But some of them succeeded nonetheless in recapturing the heavy dignity of the great Romanesque churches
of Burgundy. Holy Trinity, in Rittenhouse Square, is perhaps the most satisfying of the more academic Romanesque

Holy Trinity,
Rittenhouse Square

59

Eastern Penitentiary, now State Correctional Institution, Fairmount and Corinthian avenues

churches in Philadelphia; it possesses not only the serenity of extreme solidity but an unexpected elegance as well. In Saint Francis Xavier, at the Green Street entrance, a serious misunderstanding of the laws of proportion, an ill-considered devotion to unassimilable forms borrowed from Gothic churches of a much later era, and a taste for fantasy produced strange results. But it is a very engaging fantasy and, despite its grotesque infidelity to its ancestor, a very nearly beautiful example of latter-day Romanesque inspiration.

In the twelfth century Romanesque design was transformed into the soaring elegance of Gothic, a method of building that survived in changing forms for five hundred years in northern Europe. Gothic owes nothing in its decorative inspiration—though much in its structural engineering—to classical antecedents, a distinction it shares with modern architecture.

Pointed arches and large windows were unsuitable to the requirements of defense, and a rigorously functional variation of Gothic produced the stern castles of the Middle Ages. The starkness of what was called the "feudal style"

60

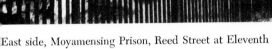
East side, Moyamensing Prison, Reed Street at Eleventh

Psi Upsilon House, University of Pennsylvania

fascinated the nineteenth century, which applied it extensively to prisons. The application was not illogical, although there is a basic difference of intention between keeping people out and keeping them in. Less intelligibly, "feudal style" was also thought suitable for university buildings.

Eastern Penitentiary (now State Correctional Institution), on Fairmount Avenue, was built 1823–36 from designs by the ubiquitous John Haviland and was a milestone in prison design. It embodied the most revolutionary ideas of prison reformers who were then trying to emend the pestilential dungeons in which criminals were generally confined. It became the principal sight for visitors to Philadelphia, and Charles Dickens is said to have come to the city with the sole purpose of inspecting it. Today outmoded, Haviland's enclosing walls remain potently suggestive. Despite the surrounding gas stations and bars, they still evoke the vision of a medieval town grimly awaiting the approach of knights and bowmen.

61

Pennsylvania Academy of Fine Arts
Broad and Cherry streets

Other attempts to construct castles in Philadelphia were less persuasive. Thomas Walter's Moyamensing Prison, started a decade after Eastern Penitentiary, suffers from triviality by comparison. More preposterous is the much later Psi Upsilon House at the university, in which the need for light and air produced large, unfeudal windows. Nothing is left to suggest military purposes except rough masonry and the sketchy crenelations from which, despite indifferent relations of town and gown, the brothers of Psi U have not yet had to defend themselves against the angry citizens of West Philadelphia with bows, arrows, or vats of molten lead.

Gothic architecture declined in power and popularity in the fifteenth century. While classicism flourished, Gothic was called barbaric. Then it caught the imagination of a generation poised on the threshold of the Romantic movement, and by the middle of the nineteenth century it was in standard use for everything from public conveniences to state capitols.

Arch Street Methodist Church

62

College Hall

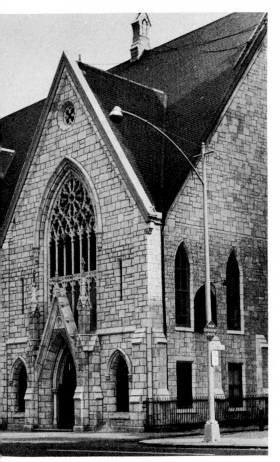

The most original architect of the neo-Gothic age to work in Philadelphia was a genius named Frank Furness. He supplemented Gothic forms with Egyptian details, classical friezes, mansard roofs, and much that was entirely his own invention; the closest affinities of his buildings are with the parlor organs designed by his contemporary Charles Eastlake. His buildings seemed bizarre and slightly eerie, even at the time they were built. But they had strong personalities and contained much sound design. The most impressive of the survivors is the Pennsylvania Academy of Fine Arts, at Broad and Cherry, a gloomy, lowering, but oddly satisfying monument, at present much in need of cleaning to uncover its polychrome glories.

Less original, and much less impressive, is College Hall, the main building of the university, designed by Thomas Richards in 1870 and built of a kind of local sandstone called serpentine, bright green in color, much admired in the period. It is now regarded with loathing by many people, and here it is tactfully covered with ivy. But the bastard Gothic forms are ineffaceable beneath the copious growth,

63

Gazebo on Lemon Hill

and the building ranks as a major and most romantic relic of unleashed enthusiasm for what Ruskin called "the architecture of truth."

More precise and less imaginative versions of Gothic were increasingly popular. In the design of the Arch Street Methodist Church experiments were scrupulously avoided, and a precise sample of a thirteenth-century French church was achieved. It is at once the most academic and most elegant Gothic church in Philadelphia.

The varied inspirations of the nineteenth century expressed themselves in remarkably varied moods. At their most lighthearted, they produced a great many small pavilions of pure whimsy, like the faintly Turkish gazebo on Lemon Hill, or the little Gothic lodges that shelter the Fairmount Park Guards against the elements. At their most portentous they produced this row of banks on Chestnut Street, west of Fourth—solemn neoclassic monuments to the intense seriousness with which Victorians regarded money.

Park Guard house, Green Street Entrance

Bank Row, Chestnut Street
between Fourth and Fifth

Logan Circle and Cathedral of SS. Peter and Paul

Masonic Temple, Penn Square

The secondhand masterpieces from past golden ages offer unending pleasure and edification to the observant. But it must be frankly said that the people who erected them very often had no idea what they were doing. They built for the pleasure they took in details more frequently than from an understanding of the effect they were having on an American industrial city. Occasionally their complacency was vindicated by time; their unsuitable models and excessive liberality in interpretation sometimes produced buildings with enough force of personality to withstand smoke, automobile traffic, adjacent skyscrapers and drastic changes in the foreground. Two Philadelphia buildings, the Roman Catholic Cathedral and the Masonic Temple, exemplify such a conquest. The one faces with massive composure the incongruous verdure and beaux-arts fountains of Logan Circle; Windrim's Masonic Temple triumphs proudly over Penn Square and the confusion of styles in which he composed it.

66

A World They Made Themselves:
Modern Philadelphia

PART THREE

By the opening of the twentieth century architects were rebelling against the pointless imitations of past ages and seeking an architecture that would harmonize with new structural methods—steel and concrete—and new needs. They evolved a theory that embodied the same architectural principles as the log cabin: form expressive of function; avoidance of mere decoration; forswearing of all imitation of the past. The modernists were against "styles." But despite themselves they fathered one, for the techniques of their buildings furnished a "language" to their followers—that is, later architects knew from the examples of the founding fathers of modernism just how they could make a building look modern.

The language of modernism became first a style and then a cliché, in precisely the fashion that neo-Georgian did. Philadelphia, always conservative, never accepted the early inspiration, of which there are no examples whatever, and was slow to accept the style. It welcomed the cliché, which is lavishly represented.

To this ungenerous generality there are exceptions. The greatest, and the oldest, example of its modern architecture is the magnificent tower of the Philadelphia Saving Fund Society. Denounced by an outraged opinion in its day, it was unanimously agreed to be revolutionary and was admired by the avant-garde as beautiful. The avant-garde was right; it has gloriously stood the test of thirty years. There are a handful of other modern buildings that vary from the fine to the interesting, in which last class may be said to belong Frank Lloyd Wright's last building, a synagogue in suburban Elkins Park which combines the qualities of a wigwam and a Japanese pagoda.

Provident Trust Co., Chestnut near Fourth

Most Philadelphians would agree that among the most conspicuous failures are the Philadelphian Apartments; the office building of the Bell Telephone Company, whose great bulk dwarfs the square before it and whose brazen siding elusively suggests something debased in the later Byzantine Empire; and the skyscrapers of Penn Center, whose bald cubes achieve the remarkable architectural feat of eliminating all trace of interest or character. There is nothing about them, not even ugliness, to attract attention.

Monumental mistakes, however, are almost as rare in modern architecture as successes. The real trouble lies not in a failure to speak the language correctly but in an attempt to speak it at all. Modern architecture has become the opposite of what it was meant to be, a force to devitalize cities and citizens. Its practitioners are just as likely as were their predecessors to overlook the surroundings of the site they are called upon to fill. They produce a series of steel-framed warehouses to shelter machines, typewriters, telephones, air conditioners, freezers, and electric stoves. Human beings, who perforce must also be sheltered, are treated by the exigencies of taste and economics as if they were also machines.

Philadelphia is much too large, and its conservatism much too strong, its devotion to single-family dwellings much too great, to have permitted the replacement of its physical structure by the vast fenestrated cubes. The New City rises in islets amid the old, with the contrasts between them always striking and sometimes picturesque. It is the conviction of real estate men—not without foundation—that the very rich like to live in large apartment houses. It is the conviction of housing authorities that lower income groups (as the poor are called now) will benefit from residence in salubrious honeycombs. The soundness of this belief is open to question, and the more enlightened planners are beginning to question it; Philadelphia, logically and blessedly, has posed more questions than other cities, which lack its endless miles of usable, solidly built single houses.

One of the most remarkable of Frank Furness's buildings was an office for the Provident Trust Company, on Chestnut Street. Now demolished, it appears here in transient comparison with an uninteresting example of the contemporary cubes that are replacing more imaginative nineteenth-century business premises.

69

Philadelphia Saving Fund Society,
Twelfth and Market streets

Log cabin, Friends' Select School,
Race Street at Sixteenth

Log cabins were the earliest functional architecture in America, barring the wigwam, the igloo, the pueblo, and the cave. Only one still exists in Philadelphia, on the grounds of Friends' Select School, at Sixteenth and Race streets. Its date is unknown, but it is at least pre-Revolutionary. The adjustment of form to function and materials is flawless.

So, in a more complex way, is that embodied in the tower of the Philadelphia Saving Fund Society, the city's oldest bank and first modern building. It was designed by William Lescaze and George Howe and finished in 1932. It has probably been more written about than any other skyscraper in the world, and more admired and reprobated. Even today, when modern architecture has become a cliché, it is easy to see some of the reasons it provoked controversy.

Interior of Women's Dormitory, University of Pennsylvania, Thirty-third and Walnut streets

Police Administration Building, Franklin Square

Medical Research Building, University of Pennsylvania

One, certainly, was its verticality (it is still the highest building in Philadelphia after City Hall), which struck conservatives as catastrophically incongruous to the low buildings around it and gave progressives the vision of a glassy spire celestially soaring, leaving behind the earthbound clutter of cheap shops and noisome traffic.

Later modern architects suffered less abuse than Lescaze, and some of them have come near to equaling his achievement. Eero Saarinen was one. Toward the end of his short career he designed a women's dormitory for the university, at Thirty-third and Walnut streets. The exterior resembles a house of detention; the interior is built around a courtyard and suggests the plaza of a small Spanish village. The contrast is intentionally astonishing, and while one may regret the grim façade turned to Walnut Street, no one could resist the enchantment of the plaza.

Louis Kahn, the most eminent of contemporary Philadelphia architects, designed the Richards Medical Research Buildings of the University of Pennsylvania in an opposite mood. They consist of a cluster of towers, reminiscent of San Gimignano. Both the grouping and the details are superb. Against the lantern of a gateway to the Jacobean quadrangles, the laboratories take on a quality both ethereal and romantic.

In still a different mood is a fourth admirable modern building, the Police Administration Building on Franklin Square. Massive and monumental, it powerfully suggests

73

Visitors' Center, Kennedy Boulevard at Sixteenth Street

exactly what it ought to suggest, the might and dignity of the state. It has, too, an affinity with ancient Rome, through no definable quality of detail or design—its serpentine conjoining of circular units is purely twentieth-century and entirely original—but by rightness of scale and impressiveness of mass.

A fondness for pavilions, characteristic of the mid-nineteenth century, is recurring, inspired perhaps by Edward Stone's United States Building at the Brussels Fair in 1958. Here is one in a light and almost flippant mood, the new visitors' center at Sixteenth Street and Kennedy Boulevard, in the Penn Center redevelopment area. Surrounded by a little park, it provides a pleasant, human note beside the deplorable, unfriendly, metallic walls of the Bell Telephone Building.

Another note of both humanity and humor is struck by the oversized clock in front of the Reading Terminal, at

74

The Philadelphian Apartments

Reading Terminal Clock and Philadelphia Saving Fund Society

Twelfth and Market streets. Seen against the marble walls of the Philadelphia Saving Fund Society, it supplies passersby not only with the time of day but with a sign of the times.

But it is rare for modern architecture to be either humane or charming. Both qualities are conspicuously absent from the Philadelphian Apartments, to which the word enormity in both of its senses is applicable. The building frowns upon the Art Museum beside it, breaks the prospect of the Parkway, offers a crushing backdrop for the dwarfed statue of Saint Joan, and half hides the agreeable bizarreries of Saint Francis Xavier's. In fairness it must be said that it represents a considerable achievement; nobody deliberately setting out to make the maximum contribution to the uglification of Philadelphia could in a lifetime of scheming have hit upon a more effective way of doing it.

75

Mole Street north

Mole Street south

Mole Street is a small thoroughfare between Fifteenth and Sixteenth streets. It has several stretches of considerable charm, interrupted by the cluster of monoliths in Penn Center, a new group of buildings on the side of abandoned railway tracks which its developers hope will become the main shopping and business center of the city. South from Race Street, Mole Street is closed by the Bell Telephone

Building; north from Ludlow Street, by the vast, faceless wall of Number 1 Penn Center Plaza. Both views provide a wholesome and ironic reminder of the difference between cities built for human beings and cities built for faceless moles. The lesson of South Mole Street is poignant: it is shortly to be demolished to make way for another office building.

Penn Center, esplanade

Penn Center and City Hall

The featureless cubes of Penn Center offer some compensating vistas in spite of themselves, or rather because of the noble efforts of city planners who saved some open space. City Hall tower, seen between them, is transformed to beauty by the contrast; and in the mist the tubbed shrubs and promenades are almost inviting. In other places, such as the high houses of the Southwark Plaza urban renewal proj-

Southwark Plaza, Emanuel Evangelical Lutheran Church, from Washington Avenue

ect, there are few compensations. The view from Washington Avenue between these lofty, hygienic holes for the underprivileged frames a Lutheran church, of odd and rather endearing design. A pious solicitude for religion preserved it from the wreckers and simultaneously stunted it, ruining the symbolism of its heaven-pointing spire.

The Way They Live:
The Row Houses

PART FOUR

Although the monoliths of the modern city rise here and there throughout the city, compared to New York or Rome, whose residential quarters consist largely of big apartment houses, Philadelphia is still overwhelmingly a low-built city, punctuated by towers as it once was—and in parts still is—punctuated by spires. The City of Homes, it proudly called itself; and it is still a city of small houses and, surprisingly, of landowners. The average person in Philadelphia lives in a house he owns; at worst he rents a room in a house that another occupant owns.

A by-product of the small houses, and a potent source of repose, is a munificent endowment of trees and gardens. Besides the carefully tended private plots, there is a variety of squares and parks. The result, for those not adhering to the belief that concrete and crowds are by definition meritorious, is charm—the charm of children flying kites in a verdant square or wading in its fountain, of old men in the sun on their benches, of quiet perspectives in the scale of people, of moments of leisure. *Dolce far niente,* a dream undreamed by most Americans, in Philadelphia is both a hope and a reality.

Row houses in West Philadelphia

The character of the city beyond its commercial center is both rustic and highly communal. The size of the dwellings imposes diffusion and contributes an almost palpable vitality to local loyalties. This balance between unity and diversity is shifting. Some neighborhoods show remarkable stability; South Philadelphia has been an Italian commune for seventy-five years and Clinton Street has been aristocratic for a hundred and fifty. But others undergo sudden transformations. In a generation Green Street has turned from upper-middle-class solidity to a Puerto Rican slum and genteel West Philadelphia has become largely a respectable middle-class Negro neighborhood. But the vigor of the neighborhood idea persists and so to a striking degree does the architectural character. Even in places where the rich have been suddenly replaced by the very poor, the outward signs of change consist more often than not in nothing more than cardboard signs in windows reading "Rooms."

Osbert Lancaster has observed that "the ability to survive drastic social reverses forms an acid test for architecture and one which it can be confidently said that housing [developments], the slums of the future, will certainly not be capable of satisfying." By this test the Philadelphia houses are triumphantly successful. When a block survives unrazed and unmodernized it invariably retains order and dignity. It may be forlorn but it is never cheap or absurd. The basic simplicity and regularity of Philadelphia houses have saved them from the outward penalties of social decay. It is only when contemporary improvements, colored tiles, imitation masonry, stainless steel, neon signs, and stucco are added that dignity yields suddenly to confusion.

This durable design was established in early colonial days and has never basically changed. The first settlers built around courtyards, but before many years had passed, the row house, economically sharing walls and presenting an unbroken façade to the street, became the common pattern. Since then there have been large variations in size and detail and some in plan, but the form is still being followed in its essentials today.

The unit, the row, forms a single architectural scheme extending for an entire block or, as Philadelphians call it, a square. There are variations, but they are generally symmetrical. The houses consist, at their simplest, of a frontage of eighteen or twenty feet, with a stair hall and three rooms, one behind another, on the ground floor. The same basic formula produced the great houses of the rich, their dimensions extended in every direction and sometimes doubled laterally to permit a central hall with drawing rooms on both sides. Such grander forms have now mostly fallen from their high estate to become roominghouses or, like the beautiful "row palaces" of Delancey Street, to be divided into expensive offices and apartments. The costs of maintenance and of servants is too high for them now; but the humbler models persist, and proliferate wherever there is open space left in the city.

The row house is extremely practical. It is cheap to build and to heat. It makes the most of expensive land while still providing the largest possible rooms plus a garden. Its chief disadvantage is that it tends to be dark, particularly in the middle part of its ground floor, but its darkness is light itself compared to most apartments in most skyscraper neighborhoods, yet it combines comfort, privacy, and economy to an extent not elsewhere equaled in urban building.

Many changes of detail are noticeable. Classical simplicity, fanlights and pilasters, yielded to more fanciful ornaments of Gothic, Renaissance or Egyptian "inspiration." Huge cornices and pediments appeared, along with plate glass. But the older forms, only slightly changed, continued side by side with the new and stylish variations. Red brick has been used consistently for row houses throughout some two hundred and seventy-five years. When its color faded, it was and is habitually *painted* over in its original color. Very often (a typically Philadelphian touch) the pointing is picked out in white paint. The aberrations of brownstone and, most deplorably, terra cotta, proved passing temptations. The only innovation that showed any staying power was a mysterious fondness for large wooden ornaments, urns or odd structures resembling bird cages, on the cornices, marking the party walls. Sometimes, where neighbors were so ill-advised as to choose different-color paints for their trims, they are bicolored. The taste for them survived for almost a hundred years.

In the period from about 1880 to 1920 bay windows were added on the second floor and porches on the first. Whole communities were built in this style, which was popular during the period of greatest expansion of housing within the city limits. The effect of the two amenities was compensatory: the bay window admitted additional light and air to the upper story, the porch excluded what there was from the first. Moreover, the front porches (usually enveloped in an absolute forest of squat classical columns) were likely to be enclosed with glass to form something weirdly entitled a "sun porch," which added a second living room at the cost of still less ventilation for the first.

After the nineteen-twenties the style began to change again. Porches and bay windows disappeared. The ground floor was elevated well above the sidewalk, as it had been earlier in more pretentious houses to provide basement kitchens and servants' quarters. Now the purpose was to admit a garage. After the Second World War developers, greatly daring, began to incorporate clichés from the modern idiom—wide windows of plate glass, a reckless and short-lived mania for glass brick, wrought-iron railings, and even "split-level treatment." The evolution continues.

But the brand-new "homes" that still rise like a vegetable growth in some tropic land across the fields of the undeveloped Northeast and in the new town of Eastwick bear a strong functional and family relationship to the original little brick houses of the colonial town. The effect on the stranger of these miles of row houses is usually startling and sometimes oppressive, but they embody the securities of privacy and ownership, and the virtues of order and harmony. They are the trade-mark of a city that still values, if often unconsciously, security and aesthetic virtue.

The row houses on Fifty-third Street date from the early twentieth century. They might have been built at any time between 1880 and 1930, when this form—the two-storied, bay-windowed, generously porched row house—was spreading over huge areas of the city. It is possible to drive for miles between street walls like these, only slightly varied by the color of the paint, the order of the columns—Etruscan columns are the commonest—and the shape of the ornaments on the rooftops—these, which resemble birdhouses, are among the most widely seen. The effect may be monotonous, but the houses are solid, comfortable, and economical; their classical details are pleasant and appropriate, and their angular alternation and repetition of triangles, squares, and cylindrical columns give a dramatic play of light and shadow.

The eighteenth-century row houses, like later ones, were adaptable to the requirements of residences both humble and grand. Artisans and shopkeepers might have lived in houses like these on Fawn Street at Panama—of a type that continued to be built for a century or more. The great men of the city had very similar, if expanded versions of the same basic design, like these on Third Street south of Chestnut.

Fawn Street at Panama Street

84

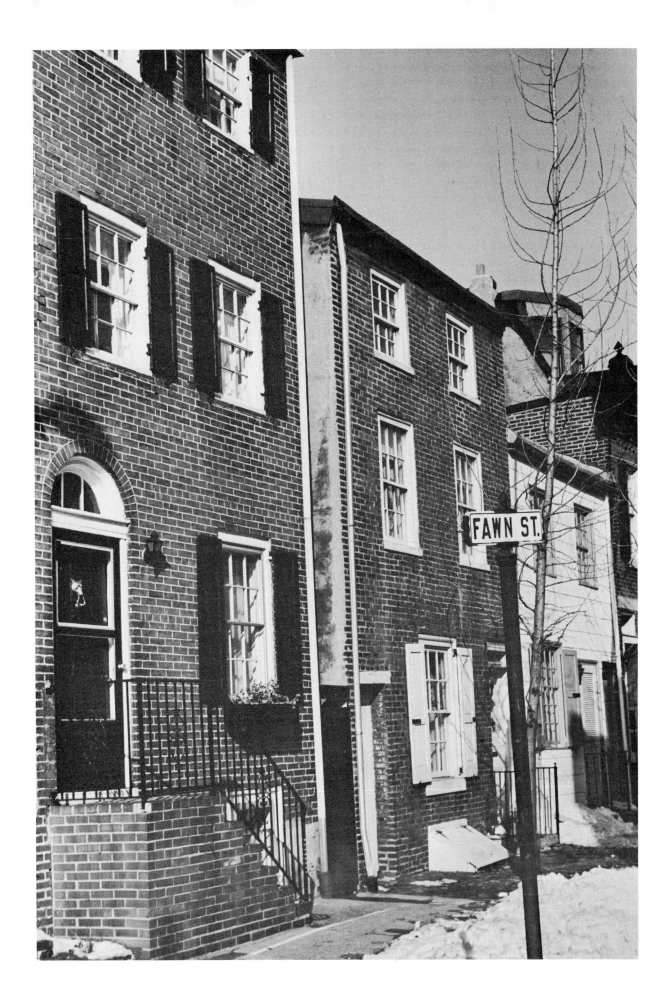

Cellar doors

Third Street houses
south of Chestnut

Row houses on North Fifteenth Street, Fairmount

One of the characteristic features of the colonial row house was the cellar doors opening to the pavement. Not until much later, when ostentation and anglophilia became fashionable, were they replaced in the residences of the rich by areaways leading to subterranean kitchens.

As the nineteenth century progressed, the population multiplied, and real estate and construction industries adjusted themselves to the need for mass housing for citizens of all classes. By 1850 groups of houses were being built on an enormous scale for speculative purposes, and uniformity succeeded the individual variations of the provincial and early republican days. A modest row on North Fifteenth Street is typical of the era. No standard design had yet been introduced, and each developer used his own judgment, but the basic outlines were perforce the same. The cheaper the house, the less elaborate, naturally, was the detail. In an age when ill-judged profusion of ornament was the curse of architecture, the poorer neighborhoods produced the best design, and an enduring dignity.

87

Modernized town houses, Addison Street

By the 1890s almost all the row houses in any given price range were being built to identical plans, whoever the developer, whatever section of the city he worked in. Not until the 1920s did individual differences recur. Philadelphians' dislike of apartments and the shortage of servants combined to speed the translation of squalid slums into high fashion, and reintroduced the notion of individual variations in the theme of modern design while still, surprisingly, retaining some sense of harmony. These on Addison Street, near Rittenhouse Square, are examples of the very numerous conversions of humble, derelict quarters near the center of the city into tiny but expensive town houses.

No example could better illustrate the astounding ability of Philadelphia houses to survive social disaster than this block of Cameron Street in Francisville. Built for respectable lower-middle-class folk, Francisville is now at the heart of a vast, dark region of rumbles, riots, and muggings called "the Jungle"—a sinister reproach to a society that has failed to solve its most immediate problems. By every consideration of sociology and economics it is the most distressing neighborhood in the city, and respectable citizens cannot

Cameron Street, Francisville

safely walk its pavements even at midday. But its houses, however insalubrious their inhabitants, their plumbing, and their appointments, give no outward indication of blight. Their solidity resists decay and their design, degradation. They stand, unaffected and unspoiled, in order and dignity, and much of the region outwardly retains a slightly picturesque, almost rustic, charm.

89

Railings on Pine Street beyond Seventh Street

Courtyard houses, Addison Street

Lantern Square

At all income levels the row houses have shown variations in the basic pattern. Throughout most of the nineteenth century the most usual form of ornament, different for each house in a square, was grillwork, whose use was singularly liberal and whose design always interesting and sometimes inspired. Unlike brick and wood, it is highly perishable, and much of it has been lost. But much remains, to form agreeable patterns like those of the railings of these middling to upper-level row houses, on Pine Street beyond Seventh.

Another, and aboriginal variation is the courtyard. It was the first form of domestic arrangement in the early city, and its use has persisted here and there in inconspicuous corners ever since, side by side with the more characteristic row. Some of the old survivors have now been converted to the needs and tastes of the modern age, in forms either quaint, like those of Lantern Square, or highly contemporary, like those of a little alcove off Addison Street. There have been a number of new ones built in recent years, a sign not of atavism but of a need to turn the backs of houses to noisy streets, and both the old and the new, scattered through the city, provide unexpected corners of unfailing interest.

91

Rittenhouse Square

Norris Square

Besides courtyards, there were always many gardens to break the rows, and open squares to break the gridiron; the five squares of Penn's plan were repeated at intervals as the city spread. Despite drastic differences in the social and economic levels of their surroundings, the open squares have much of the same atmosphere throughout Philadelphia. In Rittenhouse Square, in the center of the shopping district and surrounded by the apartments of the rich, is the same air of calm and of time agreeably wasted as in Norris Square, in working-class Kensington, where old men snooze on benches and children fly kites.

Ringgold Place is one of the few nineteenth-century examples of streets of row houses with basements above-ground. It is in a neighborhood recently reclaimed for higher income levels, where gardens and courtyards closed

93

Ringgold Place

Gate to courtyard, South Twenty-first Street at Waverly

Eastwick

by modern grilles are common. In the twentieth century, a new town is being built at Eastwick on a marshland of shantytowns at the southeastern edge of Philadelphia. Eastwick embodies the latest and most daring innovations of city planning; its chief designer is the Greek planner Constantine Doxiadis. But the houses remain themselves, faithful to the tradition of the row houses and the courtyards of eighteenth-century Philadelphia.

Eastwick

The Work They Do:
The Factory Town

PART FIVE

Philadelphia is the largest fresh-water port in the world. It handles more foreign commerce than any other in the United States. In tonnage, it is easily the second port of the nation, after New York. A great many Philadelphians are unaware of the fact that any ship ever comes to their city.

The fact is peculiar, and peculiarly representative. The economy of Philadelphia is well—and, it seems, almost deliberately—concealed. It has something over a million workers in industry in the metropolitan area. It is the headquarters of the nation's largest railroad and of a number of other large corporations. It is a major oil-refining center. It is a major banking center and the seat of the Third Federal Reserve District. It is overwhelmingly the most diversified manufacturing center in the country, if not in the world. For railroad passengers traversing the metropolitan region on their way from New York to Washington, the evidence of economic power is stunningly visible; they would not see anything like it anywhere in the country. It stretches, mile after mile of factory and refinery, from New Jersey to the Delaware border. But for many Philadelphians, and for visitors to residential suburbs or the historic shrines, the power is not merely unnoticed but unknown.

No one is unaware of economic power when he visits Pittsburgh or Detroit; its presence is not only tangible but highly publicized. The obscurity of Philadelphia's greatness is the result partly of its culture—Philadelphians are neither interested nor boastful—and partly of its structure. There are great enterprises, but characteristically they are formed of economic microcosms, of small plants, of scattered shops, of street markets and street vendors. The titans are distributed in a shady jungle of small units, and it is only along

Benjamin Franklin Bridge, from Camden

97

Former John Bromley & Co. building, Lehigh Avenue at Front Stree

the railroad tracks from north to south that their unbroken repetition gives overpowering evidence of accumulated production. The individual factories look, as often as not, like exhibits in an outdoor museum devoted to the birth of the industrial revolution. In the age of oil and electricity they cling to the banks of streams that once powered their machines. In an age of trucks they reside on railroad spurs. The harbor is discreetly edged with trees and grass; the more modern office buildings shelter behind lawns in residential suburbs. A misleadingly tranquil visage is presented to the citizens, a strange race of Americans who believe that industrial greatness is something more decorously left undiscussed.

The Benjamin Franklin Bridge—usually called the Delaware River Bridge by recalcitrant citizens for most of whom it is still *the* bridge, although there are now two others—spans the busiest part of the river. It was designed by the eminent architect Paul Cret, a resident of Philadelphia, and finished in 1926, when it was the longest bridge in the United States and was regarded as a wonder of engineering and design. Seen from the Camden shore, through the reeds on the bank, the skyline of the city opposite is still dominated by church spires, and even the passing freighters and the bridge itself do not destroy the tranquil impression that the eighteenth century is still very much alive, or reveal the maritime power of the nation's second port.

Nor do the factories generally suggest the presence of a technological revolution. Many of them are more like museums of the early age of steel and machines, of which one of the chief monuments is the textile mill of John Bromley. It is now abandoned to other purposes, but the building is an imposing memorial to the growth of industrial greatness.

Rail and road bridges, East Falls

Philadelphia's industry was based first on water power and later on coal and railroads, which usually followed the rivers, and later still on highways. Across the Schuylkill the bridge for the Roosevelt Expressway was symbolically superimposed above the old railroad bridge; and in Manayunk, along the Schuylkill Canal that carried coal down from the black country, the mills flourished in the nineteenth century in a pastoral setting. They still do: the American Container Corporation lies in the wooded valley beside the canal and the inconspicuous railroad in a setting more suited to an innocent bucolic idyl.

It was banking and retailing that financed the industry and carried its products to a mass market; and here, too, the gigantic economic growth of the nineteenth century was carried on in premises, like these wholesale houses on Arch Street, that suggested a genteel dislike of commercial display and a cultivated concern for architectural distinction.

100

Factories in Manayunk

Commercial buildings on Arch Street beyond Fourth

Oil refineries, Paschall

Even in its more modern phases, economic activity is housed in ways that seem either old-fashioned or consciously picturesque. The vertical warehouses, however uninteresting, are at least on a decently human scale. The oil refineries, cheerfully painted in pastel colors, suggest not so much raw power as a colossal colony of beehives.

Warehouses, South Philadelphia

103

Shops, East Market Street

Cheese shop, South Ninth Street Market

Fruit barrow, Ninth Street Market

Drugstore, Ninth and Race streets

To the pedestrian in almost any part of the city—and to the motorist as well—the economic life of Philadelphia misleadingly seems to consist almost entirely of the retail trade, and that on a very small scale. The assertive signs on East Market Street, beyond Sixth Street, characteristic of the largest part of the shopping districts, are entirely disproportionate to the size of the emporia they advertise. A small Italian cheese shop on South Ninth Street is typical of the intimacy—and the exotic products—the neighborhood shopper generally encounters. Philadelphians are conservative in their habits; they prefer small and long established shops, and they cling to rather old-fashioned commodities, such as live leeches purveyed in a pharmacy on Race Street. They cling, too, to old-fashioned markets where retailers sell very small quantities of goods in very small stalls, either in large covered markets or on the pavements, in the miles of open stands in the Ninth Street Market.

Cranes, Delaware Avenue

The illusion of a world of small shops is dispelled from the Pennsylvania Railroad tracks that cut through miles of factories, or by a walk along Delaware Avenue, where the forest of cranes among the docks, and the hulls of a hundred foreign ships, recount—if in hushed tones and understated statistics—the story of Philadelphia's unobtrusive economic might.

An Inheritance Claimed:
The Old City

PART SIX

When Philadelphia was the biggest and most urbane of American cities, when Benjamin Latrobe, the greatest architect of the early republic, settled there at the beginning of his career, a rich inheritance of buildings already existed. On the rising ground above Dock Creek, where Penn had landed little more than a century before, a population of some seventy thousand had already built its houses, churches, and public halls. They were simple, as accorded with the taste and tradition of the day, but opulent, as accorded with the wealth of the town. Visitors and residents alike attested the unique elegance, solidity, and sophistication of Philadelphia's urban prospects. Its beauty was considered to do credit to the city's pre-eminence, to the British civilization that had produced it, and to the Commonwealth and the republic of which it became the capital.

These wonders—the Georgian town houses, the spires, the markets and guildhalls—had a curious history in the century and a half that followed the dramatic transactions on Chestnut Street in the summer of 1776. For a generation or so afterward the center of wealth and power remained where it had been in colonial days, in a small rectangle facing the Delaware between Arch and South streets. Then, abruptly, a westward trend began. Power and wealth moved toward the Schuylkill. The new City Hall, in what Penn had called Center Square but what was still in the midst of farmland long after his death, became, belatedly, the center of the city. By then, on the eve of fashion's flight to the pastureland of West Philadelphia and to the suburbs along the new railroads, the center of elegance was in Rittenhouse Square, the center of commerce at Broad and Market. The colonial city had fallen into poverty and neglect, unvisited except by those who made their way through decaying streets to the patriotic shrines that still survived, enveloped by slums and declining enterprise. The great houses of the founding fathers (and the Tory patricians) turned into tenements and grocery stores.

The shift was remarkably sudden, and was not to be repeated. Its very abruptness averted the piecemeal destruction of the eighteenth-century town to a remarkable extent; land values fell so rapidly that the old buildings by and large survived, decrepit but miraculously conserved. Slowly decaying, the Georgian city slept out a century of oblivion.

The revival was equally sudden. The attrition of time and neglect was reversed even more rapidly than it had begun. A few Philadelphians had always been acutely conscious that they possessed an unexampled treasure encased in the spreading slum. After the Second World War, an access of municipal self-confidence and renewal induced an expanding consciousness of an asset long forgotten. The federal government, the Commonwealth of Pennsylvania, and the city embarked upon rehabilitation. A remarkable program of demolition was undertaken. Everything not Georgian was doomed; in some areas, the effect was to open transient prospects suggestive of bombed London. Everything old was to be classified, rebuilt, revived. The State House— Independence Hall, as strangers call it—was to be provided with a grandiose setting in the form of a mall cutting northward through a densely cluttered region of run-down commercial buildings. (The word mall, which originally meant a sort of croquet lawn, came by obscure steps to mean first an avenue and then any considerable open space of rectangular shape; its suitability to the vast openness that now confronts the State House is dubious.) A corresponding ruthlessness was applied to the area east of the Cradle of Liberty, where the razing skirted a handful of Buildings of Historic Interest, more or less transmogrified, and left them in unflattering isolation.

There were limitations. Many large modern buildings were torn down in this expensive emulation of Baron Haussmann (the Paris of the Second Empire provides, with morbid persistence, a model for the most deplorable of Philadelphia's bursts of beautification, City Hall being its most remarkable monument). But the largest and most modern eyesores involved an investment too considerable to permit their demolition. Thus endless numbers of small buildings, some of them of considerable interest, were torn down, but the vast and hideous Custom House remains, as do the vaster and more hideous office buildings on Independence Square, overshadowing the State House.

The intentions were good. The work of salvage and repair can merit nothing but praise. But in areas deemed to be of national importance, and therefore entrusted to the tender mercies of the federal government, the demolitions have been so wholesale, and the designation of what is historic so arbitrary, as to have disturbing effects. Buildings like Carpenters' Hall stand ghostlike in vast oceans of open space. The depredations not only involved the loss of many buildings of interest, they also frequently deformed the ones they were supposed to enhance.

But where the City of Philadelphia and its private citizens have been at work, the results are dramatically different. For the most part the National Park projects are soulless, stiff, and harrowingly formal. The area of rehabilitation, which fortunately involves most of the surviving eighteenth-century residential areas of the old city, is being worked on gradually, on a small scale, with solicitude and an eye to charm. There is some misplaced antiquarianism, and there are some questionable replacements, in the form of modern houses and apartments, for the demolished accretions of the nineteenth and twentieth centuries. But Society Hill, the name given to the old residential areas from the Free Society of Traders once established there, is on the whole a dramatic and moving success. Official Philadelphia has become a very correct and uninteresting expanse of parkland punctuated by denatured Historic Shrines. But the colonial Philadelphia of houses has become very much what it once was, a collection of small streets of great beauty emerging from the encrustations of a squalid past.

State House and Penn Mutual Building

The State House, on Chestnut Street between Fifth and Sixth, is both architecturally and historically the most important building in Philadelphia. Plans for its construction were drawn by a lawyer named Andrew Hamilton with a master carpenter named Edmund Woolley shortly after 1730, and after many delays the main building was completed by 1748. The belfry, replacing an earlier and smaller one that rotted away in the 1780s, was designed by William Strickland and built in 1828. The State House and its appendages are undoubtedly the handsomest public buildings in North America.

Signs throughout Philadelphia direct visitors to the "Historic Shrines," and Strickland's belfry is Philadelphia's emblem. But until fairly recently, most natives characteristically showed little interest in their principal attraction. Independence Hall was once put up for public sale by the city, which found it an expensive nuisance. For a time shops were installed in it. Even after Philadelphians began to realize that it constituted a commercial asset as well as a historic shrine, no one paid much attention to its setting. By the twentieth century, when furious solicitude for its welfare was awakened, it had been partly surrounded by large office buildings. The vast block of the Curtis Publishing Company on the west and the Penn Mutual Life Insurance Company on the south overwhelm Independence Square and the modest scale of the Georgian buildings. To the north, the more recent and no less ill-judged attempt by the National Park Service to create a monumental approach by razing three entire city blocks has diminished it further. But to these oversized insults, the nation's birthplace is triumphantly immune. Its flawless proportions assure its victory over mere bulk, and it still dominates its surroundings, a symbol for the survival, against large odds, of the ideas that were first set forth in it.

111

State House in fog

Library of American Philosophical Society
and Second Bank of the United States,
from Independence Square

One of the most fortunate aspects of the State House is
the small but beautiful square to the south of it. Finely
wooded, embanked above the surrounding streets, it is itself a pleasant and tranquil spot, and it frames the old
buildings with flattering verdure. To the east, through the
newly cleared lawns of the East Mall, are the Doric colon-
nade of Strickland's Second Bank of the United States,

113

Congress Hall

contemporary with the lovely belfry he designed for the State House, and the library of the American Philosophical Society, a restoration of the original building of the Library Company. To the northwest are Congress Hall, built in 1789, where the Senate and House met from 1790 to 1800, and the arcade that connects it with the State House.

East of Independence Square the federal government has injudiciously cleared another area of three city blocks, scattered through which are a group of Historic Monuments, a handful of old houses, and one or two banks and office buildings of the twentieth century. Beyond this, the city has torn down the buildings along Dock Street that were until recently the city's central food market. On their site a group of towering skyscraper apartments is being built, whose flats will overlook, as if from hovering helicopters, the city, the Historic Shrines, the Delaware with its ships, the flat reaches of southern New Jersey, and the Atlantic coast sixty miles away. The construction of these giants financed the rehabilitation of the eighteenth-century city; they are much regretted in many quarters. But they have some merits; they will make the old city again an important residential area, and their scale and design are so

Society Hill Towers and Philadelphia Merchants' Exchange

State House Arcade

radically different from anything around them that the contrast is not so much one of clashing eras as of incompatible realities. The effect of the towers beyond the silhouetted portico of Strickland's Merchants' Exchange, built in 1832, is dreamlike, and it may be optimistically interpreted as accenting the beauties of both. The Exchange is awaiting restoration, and has been shorn of the decayed bell tower that completed its exquisite symmetry. It was Strickland's masterpiece; with its semicircular porch, a lighter and more elegant reminiscence of the White House, and its curious, imaginative columns with lotus-leaf capitals, it ranks near the State House on the list of Philadelphia's treasures.

Merchants' Exchange

A site on the opposite side of the Society Hill Towers, at Second and Spruce streets, illustrates the peculiar effect of arbitrary decisions about what buildings are of historic interest. The residences of Samuel Neave and James Abercrombie, rich merchants, were built in 1789 and survived, in a degraded condition, among the accretions of later eras. As they await repairs amid the rubble, their forlorn grandeur suggests the hazards of city planning based on antiquarianism.

Old houses, Second and Spruce streets

Merchants' Exchange

Seen from close up, the mutilated Exchange shows both
its wounds and its beauty; behind it, across another stretch
of landscaped desert, is another survivor of the aesthetic
demolitions, the much older and less original Bank of the
United States. It was built from the designs of Samuel
Blodget, Jr., in the seventeen-nineties, and was inspired by
—if not copied from—the Dublin Exchange. Its prototype
endowed it with a flavor that, despite the classical affinities,
set it sharply apart from the Exchange; it is intensely
European.

Bank of the United States

The peculiarly powerful evocation of Europe—of the Dublin or London or Paris of the eighteenth century—that Blodget's bank possesses is most strongly felt beneath the columns of its great Corinthian porch. Its contrast to the native tradition, strongly felt even with the American classicism of the Exchange, is still more striking when seen beside the Pennsylvania Hospital at Eighth and Pine.

The hospital, founded in 1751 by Dr. Thomas Bond with the powerful support of Franklin, is the oldest in the country. The building was begun in 1755. The identity of its

Pennsylvania Hospital

Bank of the United States

architect is not altogether clear; whoever it may have been, he worked to great effect. The building, still in use, is a masterpiece, perhaps the second finest of the colonial period. The forms and sources are strictly English, but it was ahead of its day. It anticipated the mood, and some of the theories, of Robert Adam, five years before his first major work was begun in England. But the Pennsylvania Hospital is very American. The building, like the institution it houses, is among the most important demonstrations of a native and characteristic culture in America in the eighteenth century.

121

The Headhouse

No less native in their graceful adaptation of the English tradition that evolved out of the age of Palladianism and Christopher Wren, but much less magniloquent than the Pennsylvania Hospital, are the Pine Street Headhouse and Carpenters' Hall. Both are modest and direct by comparison with buildings like the State House or the hospital, and they give, therefore, a more accurate picture than those elabo-

Carpenters' Hall

rate public monuments of the tenor of the city's architecture at the beginning of the republican period. The Headhouse was built as part of the New Market in the first years of the nineteenth century, apparently as headquarters for a fire company, and is now the offices of the Society Hill redevelopment authority. Carpenters' Hall was, and still is, a guildhall, the home of the Carpenters' Company. It was

123

Independence Mall

Carpenters' Hall

Supreme Court and State House

built on the eve of the Revolution from the designs of an obscure but gifted man, no doubt a carpenter, named Robert Smith, and as everyone knows it was the meeting place, in 1774, of the First Continental Congress. During the occupation it became a barracks, and the British troops used its weather vane as a target for their training in marksmanship. It was the birthplace and temporary headquarters of a number of governmental and civic institutions, including the Franklin Institute and the Bank of the United States. The carpenters who still own, maintain, and meet in it are today mostly building contractors.

The demolitions that the federal government, through the hand of the National Park Service, has undertaken to convert historic Philadelphia into a smaller version of Yellowstone National Park have had the surprising result of uncovering far more ugliness than they removed. The vast malls and promenades, the large public gardens constructed on the site of buildings that fell short of the official definition of Historic frequently face the backs of city streets better left unseen. Temporarily at least, Independence Mall looks like an open wound.

Until a few years ago Carpenters' Hall stood in a courtyard narrowly surrounded by commercial buildings. Now it is seen across an open expanse, slightly softened by trees. Its beauty is more easily appreciated, but its charm and authenticity suffer. It is left like a mummy, or perhaps a tombstone, in a museum, redeemed from total lifelessness only by the fact that it alone among the Historic Shrines still serves the purpose for which it was built. The State House has had a happier fate. In Independence Square the trees are mature, and its entourage of smaller Historic Shrines still allows the kind of view, among rooftops, that its designers envisaged.

The State House belfry is the most familiar part of the building and has been duplicated widely in public buildings and even apartment houses throughout the nation. Few of the duplicators, and even fewer tourists, realize that it dates from sixty-five years after the Declaration of Independence. But it is certainly beautiful, and its Georgian mood is genuine enough, so the misapplication of patriotic fervor is unimportant; it deserves the fame it enjoys. Another prevalent patriotic misapprehension is that the Liberty Bell, which is now to be seen on the ground floor of the tower in which it once hung, was somehow involved in the ideals of the founding fathers. In fact it was cast, by loyal subjects of King George II, to commemorate the fiftieth anni-

State House belfry

Second Bank of the United States, Chestnut Street beyond Fourth

versary of Penn's Charter of Government of 1701. The inscription—"Proclaim Liberty throughout all the land unto all the inhabitants thereof"—may be regarded as prophetic, for the bell did indeed toll the Declaration of Independence, as it had for a quarter of a century tolled royal births and deaths and other events of civic interest. But its origins were not at all revolutionary. The quotation is from *Leviticus* 25:10.

The worst consequence of creating a park where a city used to be overtook Strickland's Second Bank of the United States. It was built to be seen from the ends, each of which has a Doric porch, a quasi-replica of the corresponding portion of the Parthenon. The interior of the building was entirely original, and very well designed, and the rest of the exterior consisted of perfectly blank side walls hidden by the other buildings on Chestnut and Ludlow streets.

128

Like Carpenters' Hall it has now been freed from surrounding buildings. The splendid Doric façades may be seen as they were meant to be seen with the limitations that a photograph imposes; but the visitor now must include in his view the grotesque contrast between the columned porches and the bare side walls. The consequence is an aesthetic tragedy, and an outrage to Strickland's fine conception. Appropriately, the deformed shell now houses the headquarters of the Independence National Historical Park.

In addition to buildings of Historic Interest, a number of others in the old city survived the long period of neglect, thanks to the intelligence of their owners and the efforts of local civic groups. One of the most beautiful and most important is the house on South Third Street, in the center of what was the most opulent part of the eighteenth-century city. It was built soon after the middle of the eighteenth century by Samuel Powel, a rich builder and a leader in the city's culture, who served as the last mayor under the monarchy and the first under the republic. His house was splendidly fitting to his position as first citizen. It was the scene of numerous parties attended by Washington and Lafayette. Thirty years ago it was bought by the Philadelphia Society for the Preservation of Landmarks, which also acquired and demolished a later house beside it to provide some small token of the orchards and gardens that surrounded it in the days of the Patriot Mayor.

Powel House, 244 S. Third Street

Elfreth's Alley

Pendant to the Powel House is Elfreth's Alley, an almost perfectly preserved street north of Market, the residence for the most part of humbler citizens, although it is said that both Franklin and Prince Talleyrand lived there. Some of the houses date from the 1720s, and none is later than the end of the eighteenth century. The Alley is jealously conserved by its citizens, now mostly artists and writers, but it is refreshingly shabby and unaffected, free from the deadening touch of expensive "restoration." Better than any other part of Philadelphia it shows what the eighteenth-century streets were like, narrow and intimate, lined with pleasant two- or three-story buildings; characteristic of the early city is one feature of ineffable charm, a secondary and still tinier alley opening into a little courtyard of clustered, irregular houses.

Much later and much grander than Elfreth's Alley is a fine house facing the Pennsylvania Hospital on Pine Street between Eighth and Ninth. Philadelphia was singularly rich in grillwork and wrought-iron railings; nowhere were they more effectively used to set off the chaste façade of red brick, white trim, and a classical doorway.

House on Pine Street beyond Eighth Street

House on Delancey Street beyond Second Street

Society Hill houses

Historical Commission marker

Reconstruction of Historic House

The great majority of houses in the old city, being historic only in the sense of belonging anonymously to history, fared less well than the Powel House. But in recent years they have been catalogued and registered by the Historical Commission. Buildings that bear markers like this may not be destroyed or altered without official permission: at last Philadelphians have accepted—not without many protests— the theory that antiquity is in itself a value worthy of regard. The houses of western Delancey Street, which in the nineteenth century became the best address in Philadelphia, are not immediately in need of official protection. Although few of them are still used as private houses by the wealthy, their owners are aware of the importance of maintaining them. In older areas there are historical markers. A few,

Society Hill houses

neglected and manhandled and often converted into shops, are in need of extensive remodeling to preserve or restore their original state, and are getting it. The depressing ruin opposite, at the corner of Fourth and Chestnut, has been receiving drastic therapeutic measures. More moderate doses of restoration are applied to these old houses on Delancey above Third, administered behind scaffolding erected to repoint the brick and replace the rotten window frames.

The colonial and Federal city re-emerging from the slums offers remarkable contrasts and vistas. Side by side the debased survivors and the convalescent charm subsist. Some squares are now nearly wholly restored to white trim and clean brick and colonial doorways; more often the degraded

135

Society Hill houses

and the rescued alternate, as in this square on Delancey, below Fourth. Where warehouses and even factories replaced the old houses, as they often did, they have been demolished to make way for future modern houses and apartments that share nothing with the old except scale, brick facing, and a certain harmony of philosophy. The spire of Saint Peter's rises placidly above restoration and destruction alike.

There are contrasts not only between the rescued and the derelict, but among the houses salvaged and the tech-

Society Hill houses

Society Hill houses

Powel House

niques of salvation. This block of South Third Street, above
Pine, must have contained mostly the houses of solid but
unpretentious shopkeepers and artisans; a square away is
the splendid foreporch of the Powel House. These places
are living and lively; around the corner, rising in bleak
dignity amid one of the desert-like open spaces provided by
the National Park Service, are three more fine eighteenth-
century houses which, despite the extreme care with which
they have been restored, suggest not a living city but a
funerary tribute to a dead one.

138

Reconstructed houses, Locust Street beyond Third Street

Where modern buildings—warehouses, garages, factories —have been torn down on Society Hill, they have been replaced mostly with small modern houses or with small open squares. In contrast to the empty immensity of the malls, the little parks of Society Hill enhance the charm of the old buildings and form pleasant places for relaxation among them. It is possible to wander through the whole area in small alleys and through public gardens, catching pleasant glimpses of houses restored or in the process of restoration, or of agreeable street walls.

Society Hill houses

Society Hill greenway

Society Hill houses

Reconstructed houses, Locust Street beyond Third Street

Renovated houses,
Lombard Street
at Twelfth Street

Renovated houses near Lombard Street

Pine and Camac streets

The impetus given by the Independence National Historical Park (which, whatever its shortcomings, at least showed what could be done to restore old houses) and the Society Hill redevelopment has had a remarkable effect on the rest of the city. The overscrupulous reconstruction of these houses on Locust Street has inspired less thorough but not less attractive improvements in old houses of no particular importance, far from the Historic Shrines. On Lombard Street, where many early nineteenth-century terraces survived almost unscathed in a frightful slum, islands of renewal carried out by private builders are in evidence. Some are done in deplorable taste; others, like these, are delightful.

The consequence of so large a salvage operation is to induce an impatient and covetous itchiness to carry it further. After walking along Lombard Street, it is hard to look at a building like this one, at the corner of Pine and Camac, without experiencing a strong impulse to set to work immediately with a trowel and a can of white paint.

143

Municipal Ornament:
Bronze and Water

PART SEVEN

Visitors to Philadelphia from Paris, a city of statues, are struck by the quantity (if not the quality) of statuary on the banks of the Schuylkill. Visitors from Rome are struck by the abundance of Philadelphia's supply of their own specialty, fountains.

It is difficult to know why Philadelphians should have become so massively beguiled by these twin forms of municipal ornament. Changes of regime and ideology, responsible for so much Parisian street sculpture, have been notably absent in Philadelphia. Nor did Penn's town benefit from the hydraulic skills of ancient Romans who set the style for their descendants' fountains, although Benjamin Latrobe, whose first great achievement was the municipal waterworks, may have been the author of the notion that water and art should be combined. But the beguilement is, visibly, a fact. The fondness for bronze and water developed toward the middle of the last century. It became a mania during the Civil War, an event that coincided with the extension of Fairmount Park, whose vastness provided an ample, although by no means exclusive, setting for the fruits of the beguilement. Then came the Centennial Exposition, which was erected in the park—by then the largest within the limits of any city, except for the Bois de Boulogne, which is vastly inferior in topography and, indeed, every aspect except size. The occasion inspired decoration, the wealth of the city permitted it, the passions of the Civil War and the noble memories of the Revolution encouraged it, and the tastes of the times approved it.

The mania abated very gradually. It left the city and park with an extraordinary abundance of relics. Statues of every conceivable sort abound. Statues of deceased mayors.

Waterworks

145

A statue of a tigress eating a wild boar. A statue of Joan of Arc. Statues of every known general of the Northern armies. Statues of animals from every clime. The abundance of fountains is equally staggering. Every possible design (and every known degree of pollution) is to be found. And as often as not, the two forms of self-expression were tastefully blended, the most stupendous combination being found in the Washington Monument, in front of the Art Museum—a civic festival in stone and bronze second in impressiveness only to the Albert Memorial in London, and enhanced beyond the claims of that work by water gushing from every possible source among the statuary. Water surrounds the central butte and is in turn surrounded by Red Indians, bison, moose, and a selection of Indian maidens. The décor blends other beauties, mammalian, human, and aqueous, until a lofty apex is achieved by an equestrian statue of George Washington.

The pendant to this sculptural orgy is in Logan Circle, halfway down the Parkway, where Alexander Stirling Calder worked not with Noble Sentiment and Patriotic Purpose but with a nice combination of modesty, humor, and water. Here are no large and frightening mammals but, instead, figures representing the three rivers of the city, and turtles, fish, and frogs. The effect is extremely restful by comparison.

These are the two most remarkable examples of bronze-and-water. The hundreds of lesser ones—each in its way charming, unexpected, or, at worst, unnerving—are most of them overlooked and forgotten, and sometimes left to ruin, by the contemporary citizenry. Despite their oblivion, a fondness for statuary persists. Philadelphia continues without interruption, although at a reduced rate, the process of decorating itself. An underground parking garage being built in 1964 in the square before City Hall is to be surmounted, at a cost of $500,000, by a monumental fountain with a ninety-foot basin. A whole gallery has been installed in recent years on the banks of the Schuylkill and around the Art Museum, many of its displays being sinewy tributes to the abstractions of Labor, Maternity, Science, or Social Conscience, that have replaced in public esteem the earlier ones of Courage, Religion, and Patriotism. The modern sculpture —deriving largely from Rodin who appropriately possesses a shrine of his own, an exquisite museum on the Parkway housing the casts of his great achievement—is highly controversial. Angry polemics between philistines and persons claiming Aesthetic Sensibility rage in the press whenever a new contribution is added to the massive display of Pain,

Saint Joan of Arc, Green Street and the Parkway

146

Catholic Centennial Fountain, Fairmount Park West

Peace, or Enterprise. Then the debates die, the disputed bronze or stone is left to fade into the background like a familiar picture in a parlor, and the way is opened for a new insertion into the city's singular diadem of ornament.

The fondness for fountains so marked in Philadelphia may result from preoccupation with its early and excellent water supply. Benjamin Latrobe designed the system, complete with a handsome pump house in Center Square, in the last year of the eighteenth century. The pump house is gone now, but the waterworks that Frederick Graff built a few years later on the banks of the Schuylkill, under the Fairmount reservoir, are still standing. They are overborne by the mass of the Art Museum and, having been abandoned as a waterworks and having served a term, not unfittingly, as an aquarium, they are now disused. But the series of little neo-Greek templets and pavilions is as charming as ever, and it is pleasant to imagine that they may have been the inspiration, for a population whose summer climate favors an abundant use of water, for a career of fountain building.

148

Fountain at Lemon Hill, East River Drive

Saint Joan of Arc, resplendently gilded, faces the rocky sides of the Fairmount at the end of the Parkway. It is Philadelphia's noblest statue, but it is not original. Its prototype stands in the Place des Pyramides facing the Tuileries in Paris. Like the boulevard it surveys, the statue of Saint Joan recalls the abiding Francophilia that led Philadelphians to a sporadic imitation of Parisian landmarks.

Unlike Saint Joan, the statue of Moses in Fairmount Park is completely original. It is part of a fountain erected for the Centennial of 1876 to commemorate simultaneously the part played by Roman Catholics in American history and the merits of total abstinence. This combination of tributes may seem arbitrary, but the latter is certainly appropriate to a fountain and the former is admirably achieved by large statues of eminent Catholic worthies of the past surrounding the main basin. The role of Moses in all this is conjectural, but it is he, on the peak of a large artificial crag, who dominates the proceedings.

A humbler fountain, on East River Drive at the foot of Lemon Hill, serves less elevated purposes. Its water, unlike that of many of the other fountains, is pure; and unlike that of the city water supply, it is sweet-tasting as well.

149

Remington's Cowboy, East River Drive

Saint-Gaudens' Pilgrim, East River Drive

Some of Philadelphia's statuary was carved by famous men and is of first-rate artistic importance, like Frederic Remington's Cowboy, who surveys not the range but the Schuylkill River from his pedestal above East River Drive. A near neighbor offers tribute to another region of the country: a suitably forbidding Pilgrim by Augustus Saint-Gaudens may be interpreted as a rebuke to the frivolities of Quakerism.

150

Lion Watching Over Dying Mate, zoo

Bison, Washington Monument

Animals were even more popular in the nineteenth century than symbolic humans. In front of the gates of the zoo, a distressed lion stands guard over his badly wounded mate. On the extraordinary Washington Monument at the head of the Parkway a large bison meditates on the perpetual traffic jam amid jets, pools, and competing fauna.

Moses the Law-giver, City Hall

Robert Morris

Philadelphia's native skills were most often reflected in its abundance of able, and rich, lawyers and bankers. They are not unremembered by the sculptors: on the steps of the Second Bank of the United States, Robert Morris, the financier of the Revolution, faced a row of private banks (he has since been moved to a less symbolic location) and on a high cornice of City Hall, Alexander Milne Calder's statue of Moses the Law-giver, holding the Ten Commandments, stares thoughtfully down South Broad Street.

152

Indian maiden, elk, etc., Washington Monument

On the Parkway and around the Art Museum the fountains are most numerous and entertaining. The Washington
Monument features, in addition to bison (and, of course,
Washington), elk, and Indian maidens. The monument was
the work of a German sculptor named Rudolf Siemering (it
may have been his nationality that gave rise to the rumor
that the statue of Washington is really a copy of one he
had previously done of Frederick the Great). It was presented to the city in 1896 by the Society of Cincinnati. Even
from a distance it looks peculiar.

Boris Blai's Sea Nymph

Undeterred by the indifferent success of the Washington Monument, Philadelphians have continued to encourage the combined use of statuary and water in the surroundings of the Art Museum. Boris Blai's Sea Nymph, supported by a large fish, rises from a pool on the terrace of the museum, overlooking the Parkway. On the opposite side is a very handsome fountain which the Italian Government, on the occasion of the Sesqui-Centennial Exposition in 1926, presented to the city. It is approximately modeled after one in the Borghese Gardens in Rome, and was partly destroyed by patriotic citizens during the Second World War.

Italian Fountain

Logan Circle fountains

In Logan Circle, Alexander Stirling Calder cast the pleasant figures which, spouting water, represent the three rivers, Delaware, Schuylkill, and Wissahickon. In the surrounding basin are smaller jets emerging from the mouths of frogs and turtles.

The number of fountains is so great that many of them are not only unnoticed but neglected. Here, in the East Park near the Diamond Street entrance, is a dried-up, unloved survivor of an earlier era of taste. The authors have been unable to discover the identity of the eager, if epicene, figures, or to decipher the mythological significance of the bust with the cresent-shaped tiara.

Abandoned fountain, East Park

Logan Circle fountains

157

Shakespeare Monument, Logan Circle

Laborer

While some fountains run dry, and some statues are left to crumble, the supply is constantly renewed. In front of the Free Library in Logan Circle is a black-marble monument to Shakespeare and to Philadelphia actors and actresses of the past. The monument was erected in 1928.

Along the banks of the Schuylkill is a large flagged plaza surrounded by balustrades and ornamented with groups of sculpture representing, as an ensemble, Enterprise. It contains statues of Scientist, Mother, and an enormous eagle, as well as Laborer. It dates from the second quarter of the twentieth century and was, perhaps understandably, violently criticized when it was built. No one pays much attention to it now.

At the door of the Art Museum, facing Rodin's *Six Bourgeois de Calais,* is Sir Jacob Epstein's haunting group called Social Conscience. It is undoubtedly the finest of the contemporary sculpture in the city; its peculiar beauty is emphasized rather than lost through being seen from the back, in silhouette, against the western sun.

158

Epstein's "Social Conscience"

The Familiar Details:
Things They Remember

PART EIGHT

For Philadelphians the most familiar sight after City Hall and the Parkway, and the favorite meeting place, is in a department store. This is the Eagle, a large and agreeable work in bronze in the central court of John Wanamaker's store. The store, like the Eagle, transcends the merely commercial in importance. It is an institution. In some ways it is the heart of Philadelphia. Generations of natives have grown up with a sensuous memory of the texture of the Eagle's bronze plumage and the shape of his marble pedestal —the product of long, impatient periods of waiting for tardy relatives who were to take them to lunch for a treat.

Across the aisle the store has thoughtfully provided a sort of post office, with boxes lettered alphabetically, where messages may be left by people who could not wait any longer.

Another species of fauna, also with a large clientele, is the Goat. The Goat is in Rittenhouse Square, in the center of the most expensive residential section of town. But rides on the Goat are free, and thousands of aging Philadelphians remember the shape of his horns and the agreeable sensation derived from patting his bronze hair.

A place rather similar to that of the Eagle and the Goat in the affection of natives is occupied by the Academy of Music. Its acoustics are as good as any in the world, and so is the orchestra that plays in it. The great majority of Philadelphians have never set foot in it and probably do not wish to do so. But the Academy and the Philadelphia Orchestra are recognized, almost by reflex, as constituting Philadelphia's greatest claim on the attention of the rest of the world and are regarded with loving, rather defensive pride by even the least musical citizens of a city that almost never takes pride in its accomplishments.

Wanamaker Eagle

161

Goat

A hundred other things, less prominent than the Academy or the Eagle or the Goat, are part of a Philadelphian's birthright. Homesick soldiers remember them in tropical twilights. Retired couples in Saint Petersburg dream of them. Sophisticated travelers are brought up short before a vista in Italy that suddenly recalls them. Here are a handful of them, the trade-marks and memories of Penn's town.

The Goat in Rittenhouse Square, and the Academy of Music on South Broad Street, at Locust. The Academy was designed by the eminent Napoleon Le Brun, who also contributed to the plan of the Cathedral of SS. Peter and Paul. It was located on South Broad Street so as to be remote from the noise of city traffic; it is now near the center of town. The first presentation was in 1857, a gala performance of *Il Trovatore*. Le Brun intended the exterior to be faced in stone and marble, with plenty of gilt and sculpture, but funds for this enterprise were fortunately lacking.

162

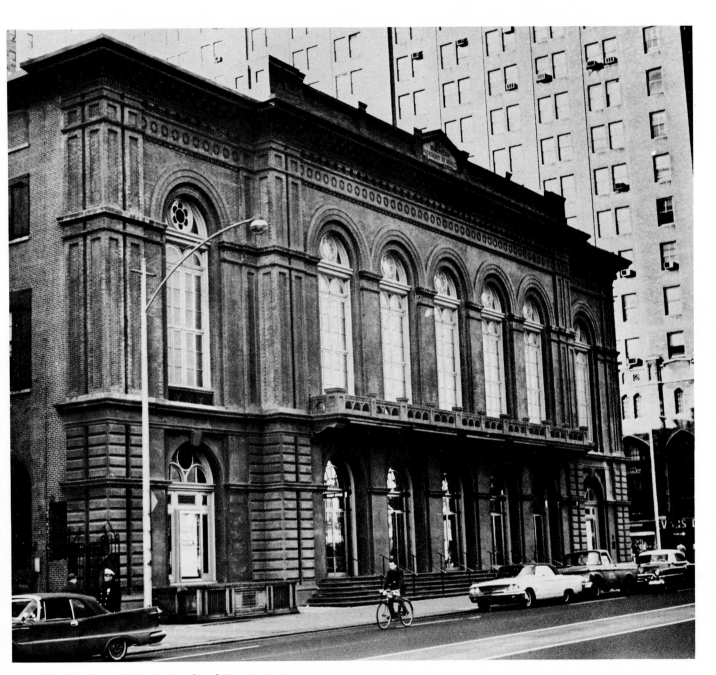

The Academy of Music, Broad and Locust streets

Park Guard house

Gate to zoo

The Park Guard houses, scattered through Fairmount Park, are much cherished. The park is administered by an autonomous and self-perpetuating commission, and the guard is entirely independent of the Philadelphia Police Force. Its members have the affable habit of returning the salutes of small children.

Having received a salute from an officer of the guard, the children may proceed, in the direction of the sign, to the zoo. It is the oldest in the United States, and one of the best. The gatehouses were designed by Frank Furness, the most original of nineteenth-century architects; having suffered for years from obloquy and neglect they are now regarded with breathless admiration by a generation for which Victorian architecture seems picturesque. The twin lodges frame a fanciful grillwork gate, through which, in season, may be seen strolling peacocks and a myna bird.

164

Gatehouse at zoo

Pine Street antique shop

Fire mark

Fire mark

Much of the peculiar quality of Philadelphia comes from the matter-of-fact survival of archaic habits. There was a time when retailers dealing in similar lines were accustomed to assemble in a single quarter of every city. The custom is now lost in most cities, except for its survival in financial centers. In Philadelphia, Pine Street from Ninth to Twelfth is almost solidly lined with antique shops. The antiques today are often somewhat tenuous, owing to a considerable excess of demand over supply. But the supply adjusts itself. Objects that might seem merely a little dated to anyone over the age of fifty are much sought after, so "Pine Street" is still a synonym for antiques on the lips of Philadelphians, and its shops still flourish. The buildings themselves share in the antiquity: here a cherub and two hitching posts are displayed for sale beyond a railing that is quite as authentic an *objet d'art*.

Two other common sorts of relics of an earlier day are perplexing to visitors. First, the fire marks, vestiges of the era of volunteer fire companies run on a profit basis, a scheme invented by Franklin. The profits came from insurance companies, also invented by Franklin, which paid the volunteers for the extinction of fires on the premises of their policyholders and which distributed metal plaques, or marks, to subscribers so that the firemen might know where to apply for rewards. It is said that there was a brisk competition among the fire companies, sometimes leading to riots. Socialism, in the form of the city fire brigade, came in 1871. The fire marks have had no function whatever since then, but thousands of them are still scrupulously maintained and freshly painted.

An even more unusual device, which, however, retains its utility to the present day, is the busybody. A busybody is a contrivance of mirrors, a sort of inverted periscope, which enables the occupants of the second-story parlor (all Philadelphia houses of any consequence have second-story parlors) to see who is ringing their doorbell without troubling to go downstairs or being seen leaning out the window. The door need not be answered if the caller is seen to be unwelcome. The effect is much the same as having a switch on the telephone bell. While busybodies are rarely installed on new houses, in older neighborhoods they are often standard equipment.

Pretzel man

Pretzels, originally a product of the Pennsylvania Dutch, are a Philadelphia specialty. Like ice cream, cinnamon buns, and pepper pot, ordinary pretzels, small and crisp, are among the Philadelphia specialties now popular throughout the nation. But *soft* pretzels, purveyed in winter in almost every square in the center of the city by pretzel men with barrows, are, like scrapple, rarely found elsewhere. They tend to be doughy.

Bookbinder's, at Second and Walnut streets, is the oldest restaurant in the city and, in a city not at all famous for

Bookbinder's Restaurant, Second and Walnut streets

good restaurants, one of the best. Like the zoo and the Academy of Music, it is very much an institution, widely favored by large families on Sunday noons. Partly because it is located at the edge of the new National Park and Society Hill, it has flourished mightily in recent years, and to its lavish Victorian premises has been added a new wing of design appropriate to the changed neighborhood, a more or less faithful Georgian pastiche. The combination is naïve but neither displeasing nor entirely inappropriate to so durable an enterprise.

Fairmount Park, cut by the slow-moving Schuylkill, is not only the largest park within the limits of any American city. It is also unique for bringing woods and fields to the very center of the town; in this respect its attractions surpass those of the more dramatic Wienerwald or the larger Bois de Boulogne. It is much frequented; anyone who has ever lived in Philadelphia has a subconscious picture of the river with its wooded hills winding through the city, a picture that may come suddenly alive if, in some museum, he comes on one of the Eakins paintings of sculls and bridges.

In the end it was, ironically, the makers of magnificence who triumphed over Penn's green country town. Their achievements, the City Hall and the Parkway, are the ones most deeply imprinted on Philadelphians' minds. However strong the tactile memory of the Eagle, however nostalgic the doughy taste of soft pretzels, however moving the prospect of the Schuylkill shore, they are less potent than the symbols of incongruous grandeur inherited from the men who failed to make a new Paris. It is at first glance a shocking paradox, for the models after which the City Hall and the Parkway were made stood for the magnificence of monarchs whose worldliness and power the Quakers excoriated.

The City Hall is in Penn Square, surmounted by Calder's vast statue of the founder, and both facts would have been as repulsive to that resolute iconoclast as the cross that hangs below his effigy in Holy Week. But the symbolism is not entirely false to his vision: the city's emblems stand also for the name he gave it, for the jumbled inadvertence of clashing traditions acclimated in a strange harmony and in mutual acceptance.

City Hall and South Broad Street

Index